ANARCHISM AND THE
MEXICAN REVOLUTION

ANARCHISM AND THE MEXICAN REVOLUTION

THE POLITICAL TRIALS OF RICARDO FLORES MAGÓN IN THE UNITED STATES

Colin M. MacLachlan

With a foreword by
John Mason Hart

University of California Press
Berkeley · Los Angeles · Oxford

University of California Press
Berkeley and Los Angeles, California

University of California Press
Oxford, England

Copyright © 1991 by
The Regents of the University of California

Library of Congress Cataloging-in-Publication Data

MacLachlan, Colin M.
 Anarchism and the Mexican Revolution: the political
trials of Ricardo Flores Magón in the United States /
Colin M. MacLachlan; with a foreword by John Mason
Hart.
  p. cm.
 Includes bibliographical references and index.
 ISBN 0–520–06928–5 (cloth).
 ISBN 0–520–07117–4 (paper).
 1. Flores Magón, Ricardo, 1873–1922. 2. Anarchism—
Southwest, New. 3. Mexicans—Southwest, New—
Politics and government. 4. Mexican Americans—
Southwest, New—Politics and government. 5. Trials
(Anarchy)—Southwest, New. 6. Mexico—Politics and
government—1910–1946. 7. United States—Politics and
government—1892–1953. I. Title.
F1234.F663M33 1991
322.4'2'092—dc20   90-42212
                                                        CIP

Printed in the United States of America

1 2 3 4 5 6 7 8 9

The paper used in this publication meets the minimum
requirements of American National Standard for Information Sciences—Permanence of Paper for Printed Library
Materials, ANSI Z39.48–1984 ∞

To Annelisa—a natural anarchist

Contents

Foreword

Ricardo Flores Magón in History

Ricardo Flores Magón, long recognized as one of the important precursors of the Mexican revolution, left an indelible stamp upon his times, his nation, and Mexicans living in the United States. In Mexico, his values, ideas and activism are constantly asserted as an example of high ideals by those involved in the contemporary political movement to criticize by contrast the present Mexican government and the political economy of that nation. Now, historical studies treating the Mexican experience in the southwestern United States indicate that Flores Magón served as a catalyst for union organizing among farm and industrial workers. Instrumental in the formation of community political consciousness and a leader in the effort to overthrow the dictatorship of Porfirio Díaz, Flores Magón became a target of the United States Justice Department.

This book is a landmark treatment of Flores Magón. It provides new information regarding the importance of his early work with Mexican and Mexican-American labor and political issues. It also demonstrates the Justice Department's belief that his radicalism constituted an internal threat because of his potential for marshaling the human and political resources of Mexicans and Mexican-Americans. Flores Magón challenged not only the authority of President Díaz in Mexico, but also the prevailing social order in both Mexico and the southwestern United States. As a result Flores Magón was incarcerated for more than half of the time between 1904 and 1922, the year he died in Leavenworth prison. The authorities did so not because of his actions directed against the

Mexican government but because of his political activities in the United States.

During the late 1890s and first decade of the twentieth century labor unrest swept the United States, prompting leading businessmen, industrialists and financiers to demand protective legislation. In 1902 the New York legislature passed the first criminal syndicalism statute providing stiff prison sentences for those who advocated the illegal or violent change of ownership of property. The law became a model for those enacted in more than forty states including California. Most of them are still operative. The criminal syndicalism laws constituted part of the larger strategy of repressing radical labor, but Mexican anarchists like Flores Magón presented a special problem. His principles appealed to one of the most oppressed segments of the working class, Spanish-speaking workers in labor-intensive sectors of the economy such as agriculture and mining, where working conditions bordered on exploitation and sometimes exceeded tolerable limits. Companies commonly employed violence against labor organizers. In 1903 the Congress and President of the United States enacted an immigration statute that banned or expelled those who advocated the overthrow of any government or did not believe in the theoretical legitimacy of the state.

In this climate of political tension, Flores Magón, his brother Enrique, and a group of avid supporters formed the Mexican Liberal Party (PLM). They advocated Mexican economic nationalism, political freedom inside Mexico, bread-and-butter labor issues such as the eight-hour day and international working-class solidarity. The Mexican ambassador to the United States, Enrique Creel of Chihuahua, lobbied against Flores Magón with the Roosevelt and Taft administrations. Creel had close ties with a number of the leading bankers of New York. One of Flores Magón's closest supporters, Manuel Sarabia, was illegally deported. A publicity campaign generated sufficient political pressure to force the government to obtain Sarabia's return.

Private detectives hired by the Mexican government, federal agents, and an assortment of local and state authorities besieged the Mexican revolutionary. At least two agents penetrated the leadership group (junta) of Flores Magón's political party. One of them represented the Furlong Detective Agency of St. Louis, which was under contract with the Mexican government to spy on the PLM. He worked in the print shop just outside the room where the junta deliberated strategies and prepared its uprisings inside Mexico, and invasions of that country from the United States. The other, John Murray, was an informant to the United States government on radical labor organizations in Mexico and the United States for most of the first two decades of the twentieth century. He sat in on junta meetings as he would later do with the Mexican Casa del Obrero Mundial, an anarchosyndicalist labor organization. In the latter case he reported his findings directly to President Woodrow Wilson.

The PLM started out in 1906 as an organization dedicated to the attainment of revolutionary political goals inside Mexico. It ended up immersed in American radicalism. The junta understandably attempted to elicit as much American moral and financial support as possible for its cause in Mexico. As a consequence American radical groups attempted to impose demands on the PLM leaders, hoping to see their policies and beliefs adopted by the Mexicans. The PLM soon came into conflict with the antisocialist trade unionists of the American Federation of Labor (AFL). Later, as suspicions of Flores Magón's anarchism grew, the socialists increasingly pressured him to clarify his political beliefs. By 1911 the PLM openly advocated communist anarchism. The most famous anarchist of his time, Prince Peter Kropotkin of Russia, corresponded with Flores Magón, complimenting him on his beliefs. Eugene V. Debs denounced the PLM's anarchy as a "fantasy."

From 1906 on the PLM leadership issued calls for revolution against the Díaz regime. Even after the regime's overthrow, Flores Magón called for continued struggle, arguing that because the national patrimony had been sold to powerful foreign and domestic interests, victory depended on socioeconomic change—not just a political reshuffling at the top.

Mexico's finest agricultural lands, mining resources, and industry had been conceded to the Guggenheim, Otis, Hearst, Rockefeller, and Morgan interests, among other foreigners. Flores Magón and the PLM rejected the new Mexican President Francisco Madero as a "revolutionary opportunist." They defined the Mexican revolution as a struggle by "proletarian multitudes" who must seize the "large territorial extensions" stolen from them by foreign and Mexican capitalists.

In 1911, acting on their beliefs, the PLM occupied several border towns, creating a short-lived anarchist foothold in Baja California. They made a point of seizing the San Ysidro Ranch in Tijuana owned by a consortium of Southern California capitalists headed by one of their arch-enemies, Harrison Gray Otis, the conservative publisher of the *Los Angeles Times*. Otis, one of the most powerful men in Southern California, helped stimulate the ensuing anti-Magonista hysteria that extended from Los Angeles to Washington, D.C., and Mexico City. Meanwhile, the Madero government launched a successful propaganda attack against the PLM forces in Baja California, calling them "filibusters."

The opposition to farm-labor organizing efforts and the politicization of Mexican workers in California and in the mineral fields of Arizona included the Phelps Dodge, National City Bank, and Anaconda-Rockefeller interests. The mixture of anarchism and Mexican nationalism proved difficult for them to understand or appreciate. Federal and state governments fully shared their antipathy, particularly as "Magonista" meetings drew ever more people from the Mexican-American community. The PLM leadership verbally and in writing linked the issues of working-class oppression in the two countries, providing both a perspective and a plan of action.

Ironically, by 1916 events inside Mexico made the Flores Magonistas and PLM a dead issue there, but in the United States rising labor unrest led by unions such as the Western Federation of Miners (WFM) and anarchosyndicalist organizations such as the Industrial Workers of the World (IWW) provoked state repression that would culminate in the destruction of radical labor during the Wilson Administration. The incarceration of so many radical American working-class leaders made the era one of the most repressive in history. During World War I, Flores Magón attempted to rally the large Mexican-American population of the Southwest against the fighting. He claimed that it was a fight between the world's leading imperialists. The federal authorities viewed the Flores Magonistas, especially Ricardo, and the PLM as a dangerous component in an emergent subversive threat to American security and the regime of private property. In 1912, 1916, and 1918, Flores Magón and his PLM co-leaders, Librado Rivera and Enrique Flores Magón, were brought to trial for their political advocacy. For their beliefs and the acts of others with whom they were associated, they became political prisoners.

This study has far-reaching implications for Mexican as well as United States history. One aspect of Mexican revolutionary historiography that has recently been under dispute is the relationship of the United States government with the factions within the revolution. Colin M. MacLachlan finds that Samuel Gompers supported revolutionary leader Venustiano Carranza in his reports to Woodrow Wilson and that Murray represented Gompers during the critical autumn of 1914 in Veracruz when the American government provided arms to the Carranza forces. This finding casts even more doubt on the dubious thesis that the United States government at any time supported the cause of Francisco Villa, whom Wilson personally considered a brigand and murderer.

The cogency of MacLachlan's message is even more impressive when one examines the sources used. The book is based on a rich mix of court records and a sweeping breadth of secondary sources. I have never seen the court records used to such great advantage in the myriad previous renderings of the Flores Magón saga. The result is a picture of government concern about the domestic American agenda of the PLM junta and the perceived need of government officials to bring the "subversives" under control. The consciousness of that need reached as high as Attorney General Thomas Watt

Gregory during the Wilson Administration and continued under President Harding.

W. F. Palmer, as the U.S. attorney, insisted upon the most stringent treatment for the Mexican prisoners—including Ricardo Flores Magón, who suffered from diabetes. His illness required constant attention, yet at McNeil Island the prison officials did little. Harassed, spied upon, his comrades illegally detained and even expelled from the United States without due process, Flores Magón was finally imprisoned at Leavenworth Federal Penitentiary. The incarceration constituted a virtual death sentence. His condition grew rapidly worse and he died in prison in 1922.

The news of his death rocked Mexico. His corpse, received at the border by President Alvaro Obregón Salido, was escorted to Mexico City by the president and was met by large crowds at various stops on the way to the capital. Eventually he received a burial with high honors in the tomb of Mexico's *hombres ilustres*. State homage to an anarchist, while incongruous, was politically necessary because the Mexican people demanded it. He was special to Mexico because he held steadfast to some of the highest ideals of Mexican culture: community independence, political freedom, economic equality, workers' control over the forces of production, national integrity, and international brotherhood. That is why, in 1968, when Mexican students and workers protested what they regarded as the corruption and lawlessness of their government in the great plaza of Mexico City, one of their leaders, while criticizing President Gustavo Díaz Ordaz, posited Ricardo Flores Magón as the alternative. He shouted "¿Fué Flores Magón un vende patria?" (Was Flores Magón a sellout?) and 250,000 voices shouted as one: . . . "No!"

—*John Mason Hart*

Acknowledgments

Research and writing beyond a certain point becomes a seren-
dipitous experience. The basic structure of a historical work
is simple enough, and one's ideas are sufficient to develop a
reasonable explanation of events. Once the completed manuscript is in hand, it is possible to contemplate the entire argument as well as to call upon friends and colleagues for critical
suggestions and personal impressions. It is at this stage that
the most off-handed observation, often expressed in a casual
setting, sets one off on an enjoyable and fruitful direction.
Books, vaguely recalled by a colleague, turn out to be crucial
to ones thesis, or some obscure comparison sparks the imagination. It is clear that *fortuna*, delivered in the form of old
friends and colleagues, eventually helps transform the basic
manuscript into a finished work. Under these circumstances
it is difficult to recall all those who have consciously or in-
advertently contributed insights or ideas. Nevertheless, certain individuals come to mind and deserve to be gratefully
acknowledged.

Old friends and fellow historians John M. Hart and Jaime
E. Rodriguez O. constantly badgered me to complete the work
and offered concrete suggestions along the way. William
Beezley, Penrose Professor of History, Lyle Brown, and
James Wilkie made detailed comments that improved the
work. Dirk Raat generously offered ideas and pertinent items
gathered in the course of his own research. Ray Sadler,
Charles Harris, and James Sandos shed light on some murky
areas of PLM activities along the border. Paul Vanderwood,
a helpful friend and colleague, read the entire manuscript and
offered excellent advice at every step of the process. Paul

Avrich, some of whose voluminous contributions to the history of anarchism appear in the bibliography, graciously read the work in draft and provided valuable suggestions. David La France helped clarify a number of confusing issues.

At Tulane friend and colleague Sam Ramer constantly made suggestions and offered encouragement all of which I greatly appreciate. Wilfred McClay and Pat Maney read the entire manuscript and offered advice. Many others provided genial conversation and amusing remarks that on reflection proved to be insightful gems. In this greatly appreciated category I want to mention Michael Boardman, Gerald Snare, Paul Lewis, Eric Mack, who also read the entire work, Dino Cinel, and Ralph Lee Woodward.

Librarians at the institutions and depositories that supplied much of the material utilized provided competent and gracious assistance that made the task much easier. Thomas Niehaus, Director of the Latin American Library at Tulane and librarian Martha Robertson offered prompt assistance. William Hendricks, director of the Sherman Foundation Library, who also has a research interest in the PLM gathered and generously made available valuable material.

The tedious but vital job of putting it all together in a typescript depended on Joan Hughes, whose good humor and cheerfulness remained intact despite innumerable revisions and second thoughts.

After such a long yet deserved listing, one well might ask what the author actually did besides drawing friends and colleagues into the enterprise. The answer is that I enjoyed the camaraderie and the sense of delight as the manuscript went through a metamorphosis under the avalanche of suggestions, assistance, and observations from so many individuals. My thanks to them all.

New Orleans   —*Colin M. MacLachlan*

1

"The Forces of Luck"

When Ricardo Flores Magón crossed the international border at Laredo, Texas, on January 4, 1904, he opened an exciting chapter in Mexico's political history. He returned in 1923, in death, unable to hear the praise and adulation accorded him as the "true precursor of the Mexican revolution." Flores Magón would have considered the battle far from won, and the official praise of the Mexican government a cruel mockery of cherished principles. Ricardo Flores Magón died an anarchist in Leavenworth Federal Penitentiary.

Born on Mexican Independence Day, September 16, 1873, in San Antonio Eloxochitlán, Oaxaca, he was a native of the same state that produced two major figures of nineteenth-century Mexican politics—Benito Juárez and Porfirio Díaz. His father, Lieutenant Colonel Teodoro Flores, fought with Juárez during the reform period, as well as against the French intervention, and had rallied to Díaz's anti-reelectionist Plan of Tuxtepec in 1876.[1] Ironically, Díaz's overthrow became Ricardo Flores Magón's obsession, and in the course of that struggle, he advanced far beyond the liberalism of Juárez. Ricardo's father may have been an Indian, although he married a mestiza, Margarita Magón.[2] Ricardo was the second of three sons, Jesús the eldest, and Enrique the youngest. The provincialism that characterized Oaxaca in the latter part of the century, together with the simple, largely communal life of its rural inhabitants, shaped Flores Magón's first view of the world.[3] Margarita Magón, the dominant force in the family, refused to allow her children to settle into the marginal existence she had known. Moving to Mexico City, she enrolled them in the Escuela Nacional Superior and subsequently in the Escuela Nacional Preparatoria and Escuela de Jurisprudencia. Limited family resources forced the boys to obtain employment in their youth; Enrique even worked as an upholsterer for one peso, twenty centavos a day. It is remarkable that Jesús actually completed his legal training.[4] Ricardo eventually dropped out of school, perhaps because he had already discovered his journalistic flair.

In 1892, the three brothers participated in student demonstrations opposing Díaz's reelection. The following year, as a member of the Centro Anti-reeleccionista, a student political organization, Ricardo helped organize a short-lived antigovernment paper, *El Democrática*. For the first time, he began to understand the risks involved in anti-Díaz agitation, and actually went into hiding in Pachuca after the paper fell victim to the government's dictatorial policies.[5] In August 1900, the three Flores Magóns, together with Antonio Horcasitas, founded the newspaper, *Regeneración*, to expose corrupt judicial practices. The newspaper soon broadened its scope, attacking all aspects of the Porfirian government.[6] On January 1, 1901, Ricardo Flores Magón attended the liberal congress in San Luis Potosí, held in response to Camilo Arriaga's manifesto calling for the reestablishment of the liberalism of Benito Juárez and the neglected Constitution of 1857. Flores Magón soon made it clear that he considered the constitution a dead issue that might require a revolution to bring about its restoration.[7] Such daring resulted in repeated arrests, imprisonment, and the total suppression of Flores Magón's increasingly scathing journalism.[8] Ricardo stepped out of Belem prison in October 1903, well aware that he faced possible death if he persisted in attacking the Díaz regime. Deprived of his weapon, the press, he went into exile in the relative safety of the United States.[9]

By the time Ricardo Flores Magón crossed the frontier into the United States the naive student protestor had become a revolutionary. He never looked the part. A man of medium height he soon became somewhat portly because of his sedentary occupation as a writer and editor. As a result his clothing always seemed a size too small and stretched slightly beyond its capabilities. He wasted little money on his wardrobe, preferring to devote his always-limited funds to more important things. Flores Magón favored conservative, even drab, colors. He appeared to be a slightly down-at-the-heels bank clerk or perhaps a genteel school teacher attempting on a skimpy budget to look neat and respectable. Ricardo's black hair reached just below his collar and curled over it, helping to camouflage the fact that he could have used a new one. The most riveting aspect of the man was his face. A large luxuriant mustache underlined and emphasized his dark, intense eyes. Glasses heightened the image that he examined the world with the burning concentration of a scientist peering through critical lenses.

Ricardo's intensity allowed for little humor. Life and the cause could not be trivialized. He saw the truth with the clear, frank certainty of the true believer. As a revolutionist he seized every opportunity to propagandize for the cause, whether he talked to an individual who had wandered into his office or whether he addressed a crowd. His deep hatred for authority stemmed in part from his provincial and marginal middle-class background. In a society that cared little about the poverty and misery of the lower classes and conceded everything to the rich, the struggle for socioeconomic betterment appeared hopelessly stacked against people like Flores Magón. While such obstacles might be overcome, as his brother Jesús demonstrated, it could only be done on an individual basis. Ricardo never forgave his older brother for abandoning the struggle for social justice while settling for his own well-being.

Ricardo Flores Magón's life revolved around the cause and he expected family and friends to demonstrate the same political dedication. One suspects that even small talk occurred only within the framework provided by his radical perspective. Constant thought, analysis, planning, and an acute awareness of hostile forces ready to crush him left little room for innocent pleasures—perhaps they might be enjoyed in the radiant future, but not now.

He lived with suppressed rage—at times surprising people

with a concerned and tightly controlled gentleness, and then shocking them with an outpouring of angry and scathing rhetoric that verbally stripped the flesh from the bone. Through unceasing intellectual labor he escaped the unhappy present into an imaginary future created by his pen. In the face of shattered dreams he continued to hope. Nevertheless, as an idealist and romantic the inevitable disappointments left him temporarily shaken and vulnerable. Ricardo's intellectual intensity coupled with emotional vulnerability attracted a loyal core of friends. He might not be able to give much in a direct emotional sense, yet he provided a focused, even mesmerizing excitement. At the same time his evident need for sympathy and understanding created a strong bond between Ricardo and a supportive inner circle. In return he offered suffering, tears, and hope. To his friends it appeared to be a reasonable exchange. Many others saw only the uncompromising revolutionary to be admired and respected as an implacable enemy of the state and the rich and powerful. To them his rhetoric had a messianic quality. His detractors and enemies shared a negative, yet equally onesided view of Ricardo.[10]

From the American side of the border, Flores Magón planned to organize resistance to Porfirio Díaz's seemingly perpetual dictatorship. To further this end, Ricardo, his brother Enrique, and a small band of fellow exiles announced the formation of the Junta Organizadora del Partido Liberal Mexicano (PLM) at St. Louis, Missouri in 1905.[11] Through their re-established newspaper, *Regeneración,* which subsequently provided innumerable pretexts for governmental harassment, they hoped to spread the spirit of resistance to the Porfirio Díaz regime on both sides of the border.[12] A liberal manifesto in 1906 set forth their goals, beginning with the re-establishment of the four-year presidential term and no immediate reelection.[13] Reformist, rather than revolutionary, the document would soon be dismissed by Flores Magón himself as a collection of timid suggestions. Among other reforms, the manifesto advocated a minimum wage, the end of child labor, and the eight-hour workday.

PLM attacks on an unresponsive state openly sympathetic to the rich and powerful, coupled with the working-class goals evident in the manifesto of 1906, placed Ricardo Flores Magón and the other members of the PLM in the same broad philosophical range as the American Left. Even Samuel Gompers's left-wing pragmatism recognized the affinity of ideas.[14] On the other extreme, anarchist Emma Goldman supported the Flores Magóns during the PLM's formative period in St. Louis and throughout the brothers' many court trials. Support, both emotional and financial, came from all sectors of the Left, which viewed the PLM struggle as part of the worldwide class conflict. The Left's basic internationalism, coupled with Flores Magón's anarchism, pressed him beyond narrow provincial concerns, and in the end, Flores Magón's manifestos addressed the "workers of the world" as well as American and Mexican labor.[15]

The connection between Mexican and American labor had historical roots predating the PLM's formation. Americans played a role in organizing railwaymen at Nuevo Laredo in 1887; at Monterrey and Puebla in 1898; and at Aguascalientes and Mexico City in 1900. In 1884 the Brotherhood of Locomotive engineers founded a Mexican local soon followed by the Order of Railway Conductors and the Brotherhood of Locomotive Firemen and Enginemen. Initially excluding Mexican labor, they eventually opened their membership to all. Nevertheless, while providing a model for union organizing, rail unions protected their American members at the expense of Mexican workers. As a result pressure mounted to Mexicanize the rail system and the government skillfully manipulated nationalistic sentiment to its advantage. Eventually in 1912 an abortive strike led to the replacement of American workers by Mexicans. Organized along craft lines American railway unions constituted a conservative influence on the Mexican workers movement. A more radical impulse came from the Western Federation of Miners, one of the most militant mining unions. The WFM established a presence in Cananea, Sonora, early in the twentieth century, as well as organized Mexican workers in Colorado and Arizona.[16] Miners paved the way for the presence and influence of the radical Industrial Workers of the World (IWW) in the Mexican labor movement. Thus, the alliance between Flores Magón and American labor, and political movements that drew upon working class support, appeared to be both natural and historical. United States government pressure on the Mexican exiles cemented those bonds.

Anarchism in its main variation rejected the concept of the state and of private property. Voluntary associations and communal assets allegedly would lead to economic justice and the elimination of poverty and associated social miseries. Opposition to capitalism rested on the belief that it exploited workers and used the state to defend its interests. Elimination of the state became a central objective. Unlike socialism, which posited a gradual move toward ownership of all property by the state as trustee for the people, anarchism called for an immediate withdrawal of worker cooperation calculated to simultaneously destroy capitalism and its instrument, the state. Education and persuasion therefore became important tools. State violence could be expected because the government functioned only to defend capitalism. Anarchism, socialism, and communism had theoretical elements in common, but parted company on the question of the state. The uneasy cooperation between the various elements of the Left stemmed from their common devotion to radical change, and the belief that others could be won over at the appropriate moment. To Ricardo Flores Magón, arriving from a country that still retained some communal land in the midst of unrestrained development by foreign capital allied with the Mexican government and the elite, anarchism provided both an explanation and a solution. In 1908 the PLM committed itself firmly, but secretly, to anarchism. Earlier, the party's newspaper, *Revolución*, which commenced publication in June 1907, carried selections from Peter Kropotkin's work and articles sympathetic to anarchist principles. During 1908, the PLM's Austin, Texas, newspaper, *Reforma, Libertad, y Justicia*, urged workers and peasants to undertake a violent revolution against capitalism.[17] For tactical reasons, however, Ricardo believed the PLM should not publicly announce its new political stance. Behind the liberal banner, he believed he could reach a large audience that otherwise might reject anarchism. The geographical move to the United States, coupled with the adoption of anarchism by the PLM's leadership, in the end proved a fatal combination. American anarchists had already become targeted by organized legal efforts to curb their activities, both real and imagined. While most followed the peaceful approach suggested by Peter Kropotkin, in the mind of the American public all anarchists were bomb-throwing madmen. Threatening rhetoric and highly publicized violence combined to confirm the stereotypical view of anarchism and heighten the irrational fear of its social impact. The fact that many immigrants professed anarchist beliefs led to its association with foreigners and the notion it represented a pernicious European import that could not be allowed to take root in American soil.

Ricardo Flores Magón struggled against a backdrop of bewildering and rapidly changing political events in Mexico as well as tumultous labor unrest, numerous waves of anti-anarchist hysteria, and repression in the United States. In the period between the collapse of the Díaz regime in 1911, and Ricardo's death in 1922, many colorful and briefly important political actors passed across the Mexican stage. Francisco León de la Barra assumed the provisional presidency with Díaz's resignation, turning it over to Francisco I. Madero after the election. President Madero's cautious approach in the face of reform demands disappointed and angered many. Indeed, his handling of labor unrest differed only in degree from that of the Díaz government, with the police and the army still being used to break strikes.

Peasant leader Emiliano Zapata violently broke with Madero, and by the end of 1912 posed a serious threat to the government. To complicate matters further, in Chihuahua Pascual Orozco rebelled against Madero. Both Zapata and Orozco called for many of the same reforms as did Ricardo Flores Magón and the PLM. A counterrevolutionary movement initiated by Félix Díaz, nephew of the deposed president, also shook the country. Madero's commander, General Victoriano Huerta, instead of putting down the threat, conspired with the United States' ambassador to seize power for himself. The unfortunate Madero died violently.

Political complexity increased with President Woodrow Wilson's policy of active intervention and the subsequent American occupation of Veracruz. After General Huerta resigned in July 1914, Carranza emerged as the most powerful political force. De facto recognition of Carranza in 1915 by the United States resulted in at least an illusion of progress toward political stability. His able military commander, Alvaro Obregón, ended Pancho Villa's military threat. Villa, in a last-ditch effort to regain the initiative, raided the American border, precipitating the punitive expedition under General John J. Pershing. Emiliano Zapata, like so many others, was assassinated. General Obregón, subsequently, turned against Carranza and forced him to flee. President Carranza in turn fell to an assassin on the road to Veracruz. General-President Obregón then began the political restructuring of the country that eventually led to its pacification.

It was during these confusing events that Ricardo sought to plan and implement his own agenda. From exile, the rapid changes made it difficult to keep abreast of the situation. Constant harassment and imprisonment in the United States tended to distort his vision as well as broaden his horizons beyond the politics of his mother country. When Flores Magón entered the United States in 1904 the struggle seemed straightforward—topple the dictatorship. It proved much more complex; Díaz's overthrow represented only the beginning of a frustrating odyssey. While Flores Magón's experience in the United States began predictably enough, it ended in Leavenworth Federal Penitentiary.

This tragic train of events was set in motion almost as soon as the exiles crossed the border. From the beginning, the activities of the small band of PLM revolutionaries concerned federal authorities anxious to remain on friendly terms with Porfirio Díaz's regime, and to avoid charges of allowing exiles to launch attacks from American sanctuaries. As a result,

Flores Magón and other PLM members soon found themselves harassed by the Furlong Detective Agency, hired by the Mexican government with State Department consent, and eventually arrested for conspiracy to violate neutrality laws. This was the first of many losing battles.

Subsequently, Flores Magón's activities became part of the history of North American radicalism, and his clashes with the courts increasingly reflected American attitudes toward internal revolutionaries. Federal trial records offer the opportunity to place Ricardo Flores Magón in the broader context of American radical history. The cases are evolutionary in that the government's motivation for prosecuting them changes from diplomatic to internal political considerations. In the end, Ricardo became a political prisoner and victim of repression, surrounded by many others convicted under the same terms and for similar reasons.[18]

Ricardo Flores Magón's involvement in some of the most fundamental libertarian questions facing the American republic, coupled with the recognition, positive as well as negative, of the United States government and of his colleagues, entitles him to an acknowledged place in American history. Moreover, in the context of current Chicano activism, he is historically important.[19] From Los Angeles, he conducted a struggle aimed at universal objectives in the grand tradition of anarchism, yet at the same time, he observed the plight of Mexicans in the United States, recognizing them as a natural constituency. Eloquently, in an article titled "In Defense of Mexicans," he wrote:

> Mexicans have been abandoned to the forces of luck in this country—akin to the way they are treated in Mexico. . . excluded from hotels and restaurants . . . found guilty and sentenced in the twinkling of an eye; the penitentiaries are full of Mexicans who are absolutely innocent. In Texas, Louisiana, and in other states they live without hope.[20]

Because of Flores Magón's concern, and his willingness to speak out against social injustice, he ranks as an important precursor of an articulated political consciousness among Mexican-Americans.[21] At the same time he continues to symbolize a principled attachment to the political ideal of social justice in a contemporary Mexico where the implied promise of the Mexican revolution of 1910 has only partially been realized. In a dramatic fashion Ricardo Flores Magón represents the historical fusion that increasingly ties the history of Mexico and the United States together.[22]

This study is not intended to be a biography of Ricardo Flores Magón, or of the Partido Liberal Mexicano; rather, it is a judicial history documenting the process of an individual harassed, reduced, and ultimately eliminated by the judicial arm of the state.

2

Arizona, 1909

Ricardo Flores Magón's difficulties with American authorities initially resulted from Mexican diplomatic pressure aimed at curbing increasingly troublesome PLM activities along the border. Both governments appreciated the disruptive economic impact of border violence. By the latter half of the nineteenth century, the distinction between Mexico's northern region and that of the American Southwest existed only in a political sense; from an economic standpoint, it appeared to be an integrated unit. The nature of the Southwest's economy changed with the passage of the mining laws of July 1866, July 1870, and May 1872. Formerly, individual prospectors roamed the area; however, the new laws favored capitalization of the industry. Legislation, coupled with railways, opened the region to large-scale operations. As historian Joseph R. Conlin observed, mining corporations followed the locomotive just as surely as in another context the flag followed the cross.[1]

In addition, the spread of electricity, following Thomas A. Edison's invention of the electric bulb, created a seemingly unlimited market for copper wire. Prospectors and small mine operators disappeared, replaced by salaried workers employed by corporations.[2] Similarly, agriculture changed after the passage of the Newlands Act of 1902. Dependent on irrigation, rail transportation, and seasonal workers, such operations required a substantial investment. Farming in the region became both capital and labor intensive. Consequently, large corporations soon dominated the region, extending across the border and exploiting the wealth of northern Mexico to satisfy economic demands centered north of the international line.

By 1910, American interests controlled three-quarters of Mexico's productive mines and many of the railway lines in northern Mexico.[3] Seasoned workers shifted back and forth from a company's Mexican operations to its American ones as the need arose. Thousands of miners moved from the Cananea, Sonora, mine, in which Anaconda had an interest, to the company's copper mines in southern Arizona. Naco, Arizona, alone had a Mexican population of more than 2,000 miners in 1908. In addition, Mexicans constituted from seventy to ninety percent of the track crews of railways in the Southwest. While the extent of the movement across the border is difficult to estimate accurately, it nevertheless appears to have been substantial. For example, between July 1908 and February 1909, Western railroad companies brought in 16,471 workers, many with prior experience on the Mexican branches of American companies.[4] In 1908, the Southern Pacific and the Atchison, Topeka, and Sante Fe each recruited more than 1,000 Mexican track hands a month.[5]

Organized labor's Samuel Gompers, well aware of the economic realities, viewed the political separation between the Southwest and northern Mexico as merely a convenient tool of international capital, designed to keep workers disunited, and insisted that such artificial divisions must be counteracted by the internationalization of labor.[6] While Gompers's initial reaction had undertones of racism directed against low-paid labor, he recognized the important implications of border development and managed to overcome his antipathy for Mexican workers. Self-interest rather than worker solidarity motivated the AFL. In 1903 the Los Angeles Central Labor Council called on the national leadership to organize migratory workers regardless of race and nationality. As they bluntly stated, such action appeared necessary as a means of protecting the American worker. Ambivalence toward such workers is evident in Gompers's response to the Oxnard sugar-beet strike that same year. Japanese workers, joined by some 400 Mexicans, won concessions. Following the victory they formed the Sugar Beet and Farm Labor's Union of Oxnard and applied for an AFL charter. Gompers was willing to accept the Mexicans, but not Japanese or Chinese. The national leadership's prejudice did not go unchallenged, but nevertheless influenced organizational efforts. Only after more radical groups entered the organizational arena did the AFL become more open. Gompers nevertheless proved to be an influential ally of the PLM at the national level and he enjoyed a political access denied radical labor leaders. The ties between the AFL and the PLM cooled after Ricardo's radicalism became evident, but in the early period Gompers provided much-needed assistance.[7]

Ricardo Flores Magón understood that border activity, including the movement of workers, automatically concerned both Mexico and the United States. Consequently, any revolutionary movement launched in the North, especially by exiles that went beyond a certain rhetorical and organizational limit, had to contend with the possibility of American repression. To head this off Ricardo sought to elicit a sympathetic neutrality from the United States government by detailing the abuses that drove him into opposition. Writing to President Theodore Roosevelt in late 1906, Flores Magón indicated the reasons he advocated the overthrow of the Díaz regime.[8] The letter stressed the undemocratic nature of Díaz's grip on the presidency through such devices as election fraud, force, and political assassination. Flores Magón charged that press censorship and manipulation of the courts by the Mexican government not only ignored the Constitution but clearly violated the basic human principle of liberty. Moreover, the conditions of the working class and its exploitation, exemplified by low wages, company stores, as well as arbitrary wage deductions, made Mexicans virtual slaves in their own land.

Flores Magón hoped that the United States government might tolerate revolutionary activity by Mexican exiles if officials could be convinced that they shared the same democratic principles. His letter went on to assure Roosevelt that, should the PLM succeed in toppling the Díaz regime, the party would restore democratic practices, serving only as a provisional government to organize a free and honest election. Supposedly, equality based on the liberal program of 1906 would end Mexico's misery, while protecting the legitimate rights of all foreigners. American aid was unnecessary, since the people, responding to PLM leadership, would bring down the oppressive dictatorship. Earnestly, Flores Magón stressed that neutrality, not intervention, served the interests of both countries.

The relatively cautious tone of Ricardo's letter to Roosevelt reflected the delicate political atmosphere in the United States in 1906. While the country traditionally served as a temporary haven where Mexican dissidents could regroup before rejoining their nation's political struggles, the situation had changed by the turn of the century. Economic development of the border region inevitably brought with it more government attention. Political stability, along the border and in Mexico, appeared both desirable and necessary to guarantee the continued and future profitability of industrial interests that spanned the international line. Those that jeopardized the existing arrangement could not be ignored.

Moreover, Flores Magón entered the United States during a period of growing official concern over the spread of anarchism. Fear of anarchism became a factor in the political response to the Haymarket riots in 1886. In 1900, an Italian member of an anarchist group in Paterson, New Jersey assassinated King Umberto of Italy.[9] Subsequently, the police attacked an anarchist rally in Chicago held to celebrate the king's violent end. On September 6, 1901 Leon F. Czolgosz, popularly believed to be an anarchist, assassinated President William McKinley. In fact, the American-born Czolgosz appears to have been mentally unbalanced, with a history of brief involvements in various political causes.[10] McKinley's assassination prompted the passage of federal and state legislation that made advocacy, opinion, and affiliation "criminal acts"; actual criminal commission was not requisite for arrest. In his first message to Congress, Theodore Roosevelt called for an all-out war against active and passive supporters of anarchism.[11] Consequently, in March 1903, Congress passed a law barring the entry of immigrants who openly advocated the overthrow of a government, as well as those who philosophically did not believe in the need for an organized state; or who associated with any organization that held such illegal views. A person who adopted anarchism within three years after entry could be deported. The Supreme Court upheld the consitutionality of the law in 1904.[12]

A number of individual states also outlawed anarchist activities. New York state's 1902 legislation subsequently became the model for the criminal syndicalism laws used to destroy the Industrial Workers of the World (IWW). Among other injunctions, it prohibited the gathering of two or more individuals for the purpose of advocating anarchism, and provided penalties for allowing their property to be used for such a gathering.[13] While the authorities invoked these laws infrequently until the 1920s, they indicated a growing restrictive tendency toward radical groups in the United States. As Robert J. Goldstein perceptively noted, such laws also marked the direct involvement of the government in the repression of radical labor. Previously, direct state action, such as police, military, and judicial force, served only as a backup for private interests.[14] Most major industrial concerns employed their own police and surveillance personnel to control labor, only calling for state help as a last resort. Increasingly, however, the government became the primary repressive instrument.

Flores Magón's cautious attempt to influence Roosevelt in this hostile political atmosphere came several months after the Cananea strike of June, 1906. A new contract, threatening layoffs as well as lower wages for Mexican labor while continuing a preferential wage and treatment policy toward Americans, resulted in three days of violence and an unknown number of deaths. Armed volunteers from Bisbee, Arizona, together with Mexican troops under Colonel Emilio Kosterlitzky, broke the strike, arrested its leaders, and conscripted miners into the army.[15] Active PLM participation in the strike appears to have been limited. However, Porfirio

Díaz preferred to view the violence as politically motivated rather than as a social response. Colonel Kosterlitzky strengthened that belief by claiming the PLM newspaper helped incite labor violence. Kosterlitzky's superior went even further, claiming that the radical Western Federation of Miners (WFM) as well as American socialists also played a role in the strike.[16]

In a similar fashion unrest in the textile industry could be blamed on external influences. The actual cause of labor conflict may be traced to cost cutting by textile companies in order to cope with overproduction and a saturated market. Reduced wages, shorter hours, and layoffs characterized the industry. Labor disputes became common. The creation of the *Gran Círculo de Obreros Libres* in 1906 represented the workers' attempt to respond to the situation. Seventy-six new organizations pressed economic issues, not abstract political or social objectives. Intransigent management virtually guaranteed labor violence. At Río Blanco the massacre (1907) of over fifty strikers at the hands of the army subsequently became a major symbol of Porfirian oppression. Nevertheless, the government at the request of both sides arranged a resolution. The PLM played a minor part in the unrest although the workers shared Flores Magón's stated goal of restoring the liberalism of Benito Juárez and the Constitution of 1857. Workers did not respond to a revolutionary ideology, nor did Ricardo Flores Magón offer one until 1911. It was tempting, however, for management to play down the bad publicity resulting from mismanagement and insensitivity to labor by suggesting the presence of radicals and implying that once these elements were dealt with tranquility would return.[17]

An important part of Porfirio Díaz's support rested on the belief that only a strongman could govern Mexico effectively. President Díaz needed and used opponents to make this point; perhaps one reason why the Flores Magóns as student agitators lived to go into exile in the United States. Labor unrest and violence, dealt with by a combination of paternalistic rhetoric, mediation, and stern repression illustrated the need for the *pan o palo* (bread or the stick) governing technique as well as demonstrated the strongman's continued utility to the

country. Similarly Ricardo Flores Magón's alleged revolutionary radicalism, as defined by the Mexican government, could
be employed to manipulate the American government, already excessively concerned with anarchism. Effective control over the extent of the political activities of Mexican exiles
depended on cooperation with American officials. At Díaz's
request, the United States Ambassador to Mexico, David E.
Thompson, sent copies of *Regeneración* to the State Department, expressing his opinion that the PLM's leaders, as dangerous anarchists, should be dealt with before they caused
more trouble. Subsequently, the attorney general received
copies of the newspaper to review in the hope that legal action could be taken. Postal authorities, both in Mexico and the
United States, removed copies of *Regeneración* and personal
correspondence from the mails in an effort to cripple PLM activities as well as to gather incriminating evidence. Over three
thousand letters fell into the hands of the Mexican consul in
St. Louis between 1906 and 1908.[18]

David P. Dyer, a United States attorney in St. Louis, began
an investigation of the PLM aimed at prosecuting them on
civil and criminal charges as well as possibly deporting Flores
Magón under the provisions of the Immigration Act of 1903.
Ambassador Thompson, who maintained direct and constant
contact with President Díaz, relayed every rumor to Washington that circulated within Mexican circles. His alarmist approach helped create a climate of concern and urgency. In
early September 1906, he informed the State Department that
a revolutionary group of some five hundred or more individuals planned to mobilize along the Arizona border and seize
control of Cananea.[19] As a result, President Roosevelt alerted
the War Department and other agencies to take precautionary
steps. Arizona Rangers, along with immigration officials, arrested suspected conspirators allegedly planning an attack
on Nogales, Sonora. Several individuals were deported, although a legal opinion clearly noted that exiles and refugees
enjoyed protection from the immigration laws.[20]

In a similar fashion, revolutionary activity in Texas also
failed. The PLM hoped to make El Paso a major staging area

for armed raids into Mexico. Strategically situated across from Ciudad Juárez, the city had a substantial Mexican population that could be rallied against the Porfirian regime. A successful seizure of Ciudad Juárez by the PLM would demonstrate the Mexican government's weakness, and provide a solid base for further activities. Before such plans were complete, informers alerted federal and local authorities, who arrested known sympathizers. Ricardo Flores Magón barely escaped by train to Los Angeles. A second attempt to organize an attack two years later suffered the same fate. Subsequently, PLM influence in El Paso declined.[21]

Arrests along the border turned up letters and instructions from the PLM's leadership that could be tied to frontier unrest and possible violations of the neutrality laws. Before federal agents decided on a course of action, the PLM's property was seized by the local sheriff in St. Louis as a result of a libel suit filed by William C. Greene, a major stockholder, along with the Anaconda Copper Company, of the Cananea mine. Ambassador Thompson, pleased with the suppression of the PLM's St. Louis newspaper, suggested that other such publications also be driven out of existence. Cooperation between federal officials and Texas subsequently led to the suppression of other suspected PLM newspapers.[22]

In spite of their concern, American authorities, however, still viewed the PLM as a threat to order, rather than as a serious revolutionary challenge to the Díaz regime. As a result, American authorities took precautionary action and willingly permitted the Mexican government to dictate the degree of pressure applied to curb the PLM. The secondary, and occasionally subservient, role of American officials in the harassment of Ricardo Flores Magón during this period may be explained by the fact that the immediate political threat appeared to be directed against the Mexican government; consequently, the sense of urgency originated in Mexico City rather than in Washington.[23]

It was not paranoia that prompted Díaz's increasingly repressive policies toward the Flores Magóns and their supporters. PLM clubs numbered over 350 scattered across the

Mexican republic, and a few armed guerrilla units under the loose control of Práxedis Guerrero had taken to the countryside. Guerrero in turn reported to the PLM leadership in the United States. Agents and supporters distributed thousands of copies of *Regeneración* in every region of the country. Even educational establishments such as the Colegio de Sonora in Hermosillo, an institution fostered by Ramón Corral, Díaz's vice-president, harbored PLM sympathizers. To make matters worse, the country's socioeconomic environment favored the regime's opponents and their political message. The collapse of the silver market led to unsettling price fluctuations, inflation, a growing national debt, and budgetary shortfalls. The peso's value in relation to the dollar continued to slide. A worldwide financial panic in 1907 forced banks to call in loans and tighten credit. Copper prices fell to ruinous levels and by the fall of 1907 unemployed miners in the states of Oaxaca, Hidalgo, Durango, Sonora, and Chihuahua roamed the streets in desperation. Thousands of laborers who had crossed into the United States to seek work returned to Mexico. All levels of Mexican society—unskilled day laborers, miners, merchants, farmers, entrepreneurs, and the wealthy—felt the impact.[24] While not necessarily ready to back a revolution, many believed that a change might be beneficial. Most thought in terms of a return to a stricter observance of long neglected liberal principles. Díaz's advancing age also encouraged speculation about the future and the possibility for change.

Porfirio Díaz understandably feared that Ricardo Flores Magón and his seemingly ubiquitous sympathizers might be able to organize and channel the widespread discontent against the regime. While little could be done about the economic situation, Díaz believed he could at least deal with the identifiable political threat. Thus, the government decided to crush the PLM's leadership rather than entertain sociopolitical compromises that might or might not defuse the social unrest. It proved to be a mistake. The revolution awaited leadership and would find it no matter how many potential leaders the government eliminated. Nevertheless, President Díaz's anti-PLM tactics on both sides of the border proved successful. Ricardo Flores Magón would be pushed into a bottomless mire of arrest, trial, and imprisonment in the United States. Flores Magón's arrest in Los Angeles set a pattern that dominated the rest of his life. Rather than a revolutionary activist he became a political martyr.

Operating under orders from Enrique Creel, the Mexican ambassador to the United States, the Furlong Detective Agency, accompanied by members of the Los Angeles police force, brought Ricardo Flores Magón to bay in Los Angeles in 1907. Ambassador Creel himself went to the West Coast to supervise the arrest and extradition of the leading member of the PLM. Thomas Furlong, acting without a warrant, arrested Ricardo Flores Magón, Librado Rivera, and Antonio I. Villarreal, conveying them, kicking and screaming, to the Los Angeles county jail. Furlong later described the arrest as sensational, but without serious injury, "except [for] a few teeth knocked out, bruised faces, and black eyes."[25]

Exactly what charges they were being held on was unclear. Criminal libel charges remained outstanding in St. Louis. In addition, the Mexican consul in Los Angeles, Antonio Lozano, requested extradition on charges of theft in excess of twenty-five dollars allegedly taken during the raid by PLM sympathizers on Jiménez, Coahuila, as well as an alleged premeditated murder on the same occasion. Linking Flores Magón with the Coahuila incident to secure extradition appears to have been a tactical error. Official reports indicated that the village treasury had lost $108.50 and a tax collector had been robbed of $15; however, the United States commissioner in San Antonio, Texas, had refused to extradite those involved in the attack on the grounds they were political rebels, not bandits. Presumably, persons indirectly involved fell into the same category.[26] Jesús Flores Magón, the eldest of the three Flores Magón brothers who remained in Mexico City, wrote President Theodore Roosevelt that extradition might well end in a death sentence for his brother Ricardo, since his offense was political, not criminal.[27] Certainly, a clear-cut case for extradition could not be made.

Enrique Creel, advised by Mexican foreign ministry lawyers, attempted to solidify official cooperation by approaching Texas state senator Frank Flink, and following his advice retained criminal lawyer Horace H. Appel as well as Judge J. G. Griner of Del Rio, Texas. United States Attorney for the Southern District of California, Oscar Lawler, who became a personal friend of "Ricky" Creel, worked closely with Mexican government representatives. After a review of the evidence, it was decided that a better case could be made against the jailed revolutionaries by connecting them with an earlier Arizona case.[28] Tomás D. Espinosa and Ildefonso R. Martínez had been indicted for neutrality law violations in Douglas, Arizona, in December 1906. The indictment charged that they acted with the encouragement of Ricardo Flores Magón, Librado Rivera, Antonio I. Villarreal, and others.

The connection of the two cases seemed obvious to a Tombstone grand jury, who duly handed down an indictment naming the three jailed PLM leaders as well as Manuel Sarabia, then at large, in spite of the fact that his name had not been connected with the Arizona case. All were charged with a conspiracy in St. Louis to initiate a military expedition against the Mexican government from the Arizona territory.[29] Bail was immediately placed at $5,000. After a hearing, the United States commissioner in Los Angeles ordered their extradition to Arizona for trial.[30] Territorial U.S. Attorney Joseph L. B. Alexander appeared certain that a conspiracy conviction could be obtained, based upon written communications from Flores Magón and the others to the Arizona revolutionaries, all of which had been placed before the U.S. commissioner in Los Angeles.

The imprisoned men, in an attempt to rally public support, issued a "Manifesto to the American People" explaining the PLM's political objectives. Carefully avoiding criticism of the American government, the manifesto's authors adopted a disappointed tone, describing themselves as somewhat bewildered over their imprisonment in the "free fatherland of Washington" after placing their faith in the fair men and women of the "goodship Mayflower." The statement evoked an image of trust, badly abused to the extent that they wondered if they had been transported to Czar Nicholas's realm, or even the "darkest heart of equatorial Africa." The manifesto traced the corruption of American justice directly to Porfirio Díaz's gold. Corrupt officials, unconcerned with the United States Constitution, thought nothing of destroying the country's institutions.

Although careful to justify their objectives within the context of the Liberal Party's 1906 platform, muted indications of the growing radicalization of the PLM leaders could be noted. The manifesto identified the PLM's cause with that of the "workers of the world," observing that the proletariat's cause knows no frontiers. That "beautiful lie," political liberty, had to be supported by a solid economic base. An organized Mexican proletariat could then play a role in the coming worldwide struggle. Allegedly, fear of the PLM's high ideals united capitalists of both countries behind the unjust imprisonment of the men. Dramatically, the prisoners called on the press to expose such a gross violation of justice. The manifesto was distributed to potentially sympathetic elements; among them, and perhaps the most receptive, was Emma Goldman, who published it in her newspaper, *Mother Earth*.[31]

The defendants managed to attract the sympathy and support of Southern California socialists, who in turn appealed to the American Socialist Party as well as to the International Socialist Bureau. In May 1908, the National Socialist Convention passed a resolution in support of Ricardo Flores Magón and his associates.[32] Prominent socialist Eugene V. Debs characterized the Mexicans as comrades in the social revolution who were being ground between two capitalist governments.[33] Labor organizations viewed the arrest and imprisonment in broad international terms. The Los Angeles Labor Council asserted that Flores Magón had been jailed because of efforts to aid the working class in general.[34] In 1908, the Denver convention of the WFM voted to provide financial aid, while the United Mine Workers (UMW) and the AFL approved supportive resolutions. Samuel Gompers and the Executive Council of the AFL, during an hour-long interview with President Theodore Roosevelt, presented a letter concerning the Los

Angeles prisoners.[35] The Political Refugee Defense League of Chicago published the letter, along with a petition for the release of the men. John Murray served as chairman of the league's Mexican Political Refugee Committee, and Jane Addams, as treasurer, received donations. Murray contacted Pennsylvania Democratic Congressman William B. Wilson, a former UMW's official who chaired the House Rules Committee, to hold a hearing on the persecution of Mexican political exiles in the United States. A congressional investigation took place in 1910.[36]

Irish-American labor organizer Mary "Mother" Jones, then in her seventies, managed to convince the UMW to vote $1,000 in aid, and raised $3,000 from other miners' organizations for trial expenses. She viewed Mexico and the United States through the same lens. To her "Díaz and Harriman and Rockefeller and the whole push (sic) are together down there . . . wining and dining, and we paid for it." Mother Jones likened the imprisoned men to such patriots as Guiseppe Garibaldi and George Washington, declaring that the Mexicans fought against a tyrant bloodier than King George.[37] In a meeting with President William Howard Taft, she pleaded for the release of the Mexican prisoners, causing the President to remark that if she had her way, there would not be anyone left in the penitentiaries. Spiritedly, Mother Jones rejoined that if the United States devoted half the money it spent on prisons toward providing decent social and economic opportunities, there would be fewer men to pardon.[38]

In Los Angeles, a small group of socialists formed a Mexican Revolutionists Defense League. Among them were John Kenneth Turner, author of the exposé *Barbarous Mexico*, which first appeared in the *American Magazine* in 1909, and a year later in the *Appeal to Reason*; and John Murray, already active in defense of the PLM.[39] Turner's avid support of Ricardo Flores Magón prompted a federal investigation into his background. For a brief period, the government believed that an English anarchist named John Turner, who had been ordered deported in 1903, and John Kenneth Turner were one and the same. After an extensive investigation, the Justice Department regretfully concluded they were not, and dropped the idea of instituting deportation proceedings against him.[40] Elizabeth Darling Trowbridge, a Boston millionairess turned socialist, underwrote the group's expenses. Miss Trowbridge later married Manuel Sarabia, romantically spiriting him off to England to escape American authorities and the years of imprisonment that befell other members of the PLM.[41]

The *Appeal to Reason*, one of the most influential socialist newspapers in the United States, devoted almost all of its March 13, 1909, issue to the PLM. Prominently featured on the front page, in bold print, was Flores Magón's statement that the government refused to allow the prisoners to read the *Appeal*. A lead article, bearing Flores Magón's name, set forth the reasons for their imprisonment, and described their treatment in the Los Angeles County jail. The imprisoned men were not permitted access to books and newspapers, or even to receive letters. To enforce such rules, the jailers, as well as federal attorney Oscar Lawler, searched all visitors. Flores Magón charged that women sympathizers were abused and embarrassed in the process. Lawler, according to Flores Magón, ran his hands over Rivera's young wife under the pretext of searching for forbidden communications. Sadly, Ricardo noted that he would have expected as much in Mexico, but certainly not in the United States. The article concluded with a statement on the vital importance of American public opinion.[42]

The *Appeal*'s editors dramatically refused to explain how Flores Magón had written and delivered his story. Lawler justified holding the men incommunicado by citing a series of articles in the local Hearst newspaper, the *Examiner*, which claimed that Flores Magón directed border violence from his jail cell. Unknown to the imprisoned men, Antonio Lozano, the Mexican consul, had photographed the personal letters and messages that they had laboriously written on strips of cloth and sewn into their dirty laundry. In a similar fashion, incoming messages reached their hands only after being photographed. Both Lawler and the Mexican ministry of foreign relations received copies.[43]

The *Appeal to Reason*'s campaign provoked sharp reactions from federal officials. Oscar Lawler blamed the *Appeal* for inspiring a number of threatening letters addressed to federal officers.[44] In Las Cruces, New Mexico, the federal attorney's office suggested that the newspaper's editor used the Mexican case as a fund-raising ploy, and in their intemperate zeal, they had strayed into the area of nonmailable materials.[45] The official attacks on the PLM stimulated sympathetic support from all over the nation. In San Antonio, Texas, a circular equated the Flores Magón case with the direct interests of both the Mexican and American worker. The international border was dismissed as merely an imaginary line.[46] A group of "ladies and young ladies" in Rotan, Texas, issued a supportive statement.[47] From Shreveport, Louisiana, Local 215 of the Women's International Union Label League wrote to Attorney General George W. Wickersham, protesting the imprisonment of these Mexican friends of organized labor.[48]

Given the Left's numerical and political weakness, such an outpouring of concern appears more impressive on paper than it was in actual fact. It did, however, have the effect of altering and broadening Ricardo Flores Magón's cause beyond the immediate concerns of Mexican politics. An appeal for funds distributed by Modesto Díaz symbolically marked the merging of the Mexican cause with the American Left's international interests. Listed as supporting the aid request were the PLM; the Los Angeles County Socialist Party; the Socialist Workers Party of Los Angeles; the Industrial Workers of the World, No. 12; the Los Angeles Social Sciences Club; and the Socialist Party, Mexican section.[49]

When the time came, Job Harriman and A. R. Holston, two well-known socialist lawyers, led the defense.[50] They managed to delay extradition for over a year-and-a-half by appealing to the Supreme Court, while the defendants, unable to post bond, remained in the Los Angeles county jail as political martyrs.[51] Finally, in March 1909, a United States marshal delivered them to Arizona to stand trial. The extradition fight, as well as the various appeals made to the president, congress, and the attorney general, assured the politicization of the proceedings far beyond the original considerations of the United States government. Consequently, Attorney General Charles J. Bonaparte warned Territorial Attorney Alexander against any illegal deportations. Many PLM supporters believed that the government intended to permit the prisoners to be kidnapped and spirited across the border to be dealt with by Mexican authorities.[52] The publicity focused on the case obviously made it more complicated to handle.

Alexander's response appears to be one of the first official attempts to link Ricardo Flores Magón to the broad currents of American political radicalism. The United States territorial attorney characterized the PLM as rank anarchists and socialists defended by an "anarchistically inclined" socialist lawyer.[53] A previous suggestion that the defendants could be associated with political extremism arose during the hearing before the U.S. commissioner in Los Angeles, when the significance of a red flag seized in the raid on the headquarters of the Arizona revolutionaries had been discussed, although the witness denied any connection between the flag's color and anarchism. Alexander's reformulation advanced the process of moving PLM activities from a neutrality act question to a more serious internal issue. During the period that the Flores Magóns remained in jail, another anarchist scare swept the country. In the spring of 1908 a number of sensational events had been attributed to anarchists. The murder of a Denver priest, an attempt on the life of Chicago's police chief, and a bombing in New York's Union Square that barely missed being a massacre caused official concern. An alarmed President Roosevelt demanded stiffer laws and a ban on anarchist publications from the unsealed mails. Federal immigration officers received orders to cooperate with local police departments in the rounding up and deportation of alien anarchists. Alexander undoubtedly had been urged to view the PLM as a dangerous anarchist organization by Mexican government representatives. The Díaz regime had long charged that its opponents were revolutionary anarchists and, as previously noted, U.S. Ambassador David E. Thompson conveyed that view in his correspondence with the State Department.[54]

The danger of some sort of radical political contamination on the border resulting from the presence of PLM's leadership in the United States clearly concerned federal authorities. Their uneasiness could only have been heightened by the March 27, 1909, edition of the *Appeal to Reason*. The *Appeal* carried a front-page manifesto addressed to the working class of America. Representing the editorial staff's opinion, rather than that of Ricardo Flores Magón, the paper noted the connection between events in Mexico and the United States. The *Appeal* observed that American plutocrats desired the suppression of the PLM as much as President Díaz. The recent jailing of Samuel Gompers of the AFL, as well as Flores Magón, appeared to be part of the same pattern. In bold type, the manifesto declared that a true understanding of the Mexican situation would provoke a revolution in the United States. According to the *Appeal*, persecution of the PLM offered the greatest opportunity ever for sweeping the workers' apathy away, and moving on to a working-class victory. Rather prematurely, George H. Shoaf, staff correspondent, offered a hurrah for the "international revolutionary movement," boldly declaring that border warfare involved both the American worker and the Mexican peon.[55] The *Appeal to Reason* obviously overstated the extent of working-class interest as well as overestimated concern over Flores Magón's imprisonment; nevertheless, the editors presented the PLM's activities as part of a worldwide struggle with a potential for leading the United States into a class revolution. Such published dreams hardened the government's resolve to deal and dispense with the PLM problem as effectively as possible.

In Tucson, the defendants relied upon labor union lawyers William B. Cleary and A. A. Worsley, whose fees were paid in part by the WFM and the Political Refugee Defense League of Chicago. Coming to Flores Magón's aid was a natural extension of the WFM tactic of aggressively recruiting Mexican labor. Several PLM leaders in Arizona belonged to the WFM and also distributed IWW pamphlets. Attracting Mexican members and demonstrating support for the PLM fitted in with the WFM's grand strategy of overwhelming the AFL. Union lawyer Cleary subsequently helped defend the IWW's leadership, including Bill Haywood, following a federal raid on the Chicago headquarters and its branches in September of 1917.[56] The PLM case formed part of his apprenticeship in the struggle against political repression. Unfortunately, the letters and instructions sent by the PLM leaders to the Arizona revolutionaries prior to their arrest proved damaging evidence. Over defense objections, the government introduced documentary evidence, obtained by the Arizona Rangers during a raid on the Douglas PLM supporters, which outlined the seizure of custom houses and other public buildings on the Mexican side of the border. Little room remained to claim semantic differences; as a result, the defense fell back on technicalities, alleging that the grand jury had no legal grounds to issue an indictment because the offense the defendants were charged with—conspiracy—did not fall within the court's jurisdiction or that of the Second Judicial District of the Territory of Arizona.

Cleary asserted it could not be proven that the letters and instructions had originated in American territory. Moreover, the defense claimed that the charge itself appeared vague, resulting in the conspiracy violation's being mixed with the actual offense of initiating a military expedition. Since the defendants had not set foot in Arizona, the connection could not be made.[57] The defense characterized the trial as one actually directed against the American labor movement through Flores Magón, known to be a supporter and friend of American labor. At the very beginning of the trial the defense emphasized the connection between Flores Magón and labor by probing prospective jurors for their views of the militant WFM. Ironically, the WFM used Flores Magón's plight for its own purposes attempting to present the union as the main target and thus acquire some painless martyrdom at the expense of the PLM's leadership. Ricardo's objective, the over-

throw of Porfirio Díaz, had been overshadowed by his bene-
factors. U.S. Attorney Alexander tried to steer clear of the
ideological trap set up by the WFM's lawyers and presented
the issue as a case of simple criminal violence. He asserted
that rather than patriots the PLM leaders were parasitic "graft-
ers" supported by deluded persons, and that the United States
"is no place in which to harbor criminals."[58]

Evidently, even before the jury announced the decision,
the verdict had been revealed to officials and Mexican government observers. Despite a great deal of speculation concerning the outcome, including rumors of a hung jury, the jurors
reached a guilty verdict. When the jury publicly returned the
verdict, only PLM friends and supporters were surprised.
The judge speedily rejected Cleary's motion for a new trial
and notice of appeal.[59] The government was relieved and
gratified by the result; however, they had already laid con-
tingency plans in the event federal authorities failed to prove
the Arizona case. An outstanding indictment in Texas could
have been utilized to keep the men in custody pending
another trial, if necessary. In fact, there had been some discussion as to whether or not it might be advantageous to have
the case tried in Texas anyway. Only Alexander's earnest as-
surances that he could produce a conviction, an opinion supported by Lawler, persuaded the Justice Department to allow
the Arizona proceedings to continue. Bonaparte's successor,
Attorney General George W. Wickersham, was determined to
send the men to prison under one conviction or another. Well
aware of the Mexican government's concern, as well as that
of the United States Department of State, he kept the Mexican
Embassy in Washington, D.C., fully informed of his inten-
tions and the latest developments.[60] Subsequently, the convicted men received eighteen-month terms in territorial
prison.[61] An appeal to the territorial supreme court failed, as
did a petition to President William Howard Taft.

The most significant result of the Arizona trial was not the
temporary removal of troublesome revolutionaries, although
the Mexican government approved of the sentence. More importantly, the PLM junta had been linked to American

radicalism. Having begun the judicial process identified with Mexican affairs, the PLM ended it linked with American internal political concerns.

Finally, on August 3, 1910, almost exactly three years after their arrest, the imprisoned men walked out of Florence Penitentiary to be greeted by John Kenneth Turner and a group representing the WFM. Ethel Duffy Turner implies in her account that they made a conscious effort to demonstrate to the freed men that, far from being politically isolated, supporters and sympathizers remained.[62] Still suffering psychologically from their first major brush with the American judicial system, such support could only have been reassuring. On their arrival in Los Angeles, a large crowd met them at the station with flowers and cheers. Several nights later, an emotional mass meeting at the Labor Temple formally marked Flores Magón's return to the broader social struggle. Presided over by socialist lawyer A. R. Holston, the meeting featured a lecture by John Kenneth Turner describing the persecution of the PLM on American soil, and a review of the legal aspects by Job Harriman. Antonio Villarreal pledged to continue the struggle, while Ricardo, enormously buoyed by the occasion, led the *vivas* for "*la revolución social.*" Enthusiastic supporters contributed $414 to help re-establish *Regeneración*—it seemed to be a good start toward revival.[63]

While Flores Magón's move into radical politics appears obvious after the 1907 Los Angeles arrest, his anarchism made it difficult for him to work with the American Left, despite the fact the beleaguered Mexicans so desperately needed allies. One detects a degree of hostility in his relations with the Left—a reaction to his dependence on them coupled with his frustration that they did not do more to assist the revolution as defined by the PLM's leadership. Even though Flores Magón understood that his radical friends and allies had their own agenda that did not necessarily complement fully that of the PLM, in exasperation, he called the socialists cowards, and ridiculed the AFL. Moreover, Flores Magón, as an intellectual, found the condescending nature of much of the assistance annoying. The stereotype of the Mexican worker as an illiterate peasant certainly did not apply to the PLM's leadership, yet such an image persisted. With reason, Flores Magón complained that few realized that the PLM, in spite of poverty and brown skins, "had nerves, a heart, and a brain."[64]

Flores Magón found support from anarchists much more acceptable. Emma Goldman shared the PLM's belief that Mexico constituted an important arena in the coming worldwide struggle; accordingly, her newspaper consistently devoted considerable space to Mexican affairs.[65] Even with Ricardo temporarily out of circulation in Florence Penitentiary, Goldman continued with anti-Díaz activities. When Carlos de Fornaro's polemical book, *Díaz, Czar of Mexico* (1909), resulted in the trial and imprisonment of the New York artist on libel charges, *Mother Earth* commented editorially on the remarkable ability of the "Mexican beast" to scent its prey from afar with the result that many Mexican patriots languished in American jails.[66]

On the other hand, socialist Eugene V. Debs, who, in retrospect, offered sound advice, cautioned the PLM to be content with slowly laying the foundation for change rather than pushing capitalism into an open conflict. He noted that the enslaved working class could not be relied upon, whether in the United States or Europe, to provide effective aid. To Debs, as a socialist, the PLM's dream of a Mexican "Anarchist-communism" seemed a flight of fancy—an assessment Flores Magón could not accept gracefully.[67] Nevertheless, although it was a struggle and required restraint and patience, Flores Magón believed that Mexican anarchists had to "cultivate international relations" with workers' organizations, whether they were trade unionists, socialists, or anarchists, in all parts of the world.[68] With such wide support, the PLM's revolution might well become the beginning of a wider anarchist movement involving Mexican and American workers in the Southwest.

3

Los Angeles, 1912

On the eve of the Mexican revolution, Ricardo Flores Magón's political ideas and goals had evolved far beyond the liberal platform of 1906, yet, he decided not to openly and aggressively convey his new radical ideas to his Mexican followers. Ricardo relied upon local initiative to found PLM clubs and organizations. The numerous groups that had sprouted up throughout the country functioned without much direction and each group responded to the political reality as it saw fit. The fact that the PLM's platform of 1906 offered traditional liberal remedies, with only a few radical modifications, made the philosophical differences between Flores Magón and Francisco Madero appear minor. One could be a member of a local PLM club and also support Madero. Ironically, many PLM organizations and their members would have preferred a more radical approach. Ricardo's 1911 program, had it been announced much earlier, might well have held his followers together. In its absence many of his supporters chose to read into Madero's mild reformism the more far-reaching changes they wanted to see. Flores Magón's muted and disguised internationalistic anarchism while exiled, made it difficult to politically differentiate the PLM from other opponents of the Díaz regime. To the PLM leadership, however, Madero represented just another face within the capitalist class; consequently, an alliance with Madero's forces against Porfirio Díaz was inconceivable, especially in view of the PLM's fond hope that Mexico would produce the spark that would set off a worldwide revolution. While Madero thought in narrow nationalistic terms and sought to serve as a traditional president, Flores Magón believed the struggle required a fundamental adjustment of social classes that transcended a single country. It remained a private vision rather than a rallying point. The almost casual political disintegration of the PLM within Mexico is exemplified by the experience of the anti-Díaz forces in the important state of Puebla. Most of the opponents of the dictatorship had ties with Flores Magón. Hilario C. Salas, a former factory worker in Orizaba (Veracruz) led an abortive PLM uprising in 1906. Sales also belonged to the traditional liberal club *Regeneración*. Juan Cuamatzi, a member of the same club and a former head of the municipal council of San Bernardino Contla had joined the PLM in 1907 along with most of his village. Indeed, at one point virtually all anti-Díaz activity in Puebla was associated with the Magonistas. The drift away from the PLM and the acceptance of Madero's leadership was facilitated by people like Aquiles Serdán. A shoemaker from a previously well-to-do family, Serdán believed that Madero could provide the framework within which more radical solutions might be pushed forward. His father, Manuel Serdán, had been involved with an anarchist group in 1878. Aquiles's father disappeared after a series of rebellions—probably the victim of a political assassination. Serdán's shop became the meeting place for anti-Díaz activists, including workers and students—most of whom had PLM ties. In reality Serdán's radicalism matched that of Flores Magón, nevertheless he became the chief Maderista leader in his state.[1] The PLM's political strategy prior to 1911 failed to harness what can only be described as a natural constituency. Flores Magón's supporters in other parts of Mexico and in the United States experienced a similar process of drift and detachment from the PLM in an operational sense. The other active participants in the Mexican revolution created a sense of excitement, movement, and hope that the PLM could not match, especially with its outmoded 1906 platform.

Ricardo's timetable for an armed PLM offensive within Mexico repeatedly had been thrown off schedule by raids and arrests. He became concerned about the possibility of American intervention in Mexico that might abort the entire revolutionary process. Writing to Samuel Gompers in March

1911, he asked for support against the "money powers": Standard Oil Company, the Guggenheims, Southern Pacific Railway, the sugar trust, and all the "Wall Street Autocracy," reportedly pressing for armed intervention in Mexico. If the workers organized by the AFL spoke out, it would help counterbalance the pressure on the government to meddle. Several days later, a similar appeal was sent to Emma Goldman. Ricardo's growing sophistication and understanding of the North American Left were indicated by his closing salutations: the letter to Gompers closed with the phrase, "Yours for human liberty," while that to Goldman went further, ending with "Yours for human emancipation."[2]

The most heartening reaction came from the socialist press, which responded to the threat of American intervention with enthusiastic alarm. Both the *Appeal to Reason* and the *New York Call* consistently demanded that the United States adopt a non-interventionist policy in opposition to the alleged pressure of American capitalists for action. While they could hardly claim to have succeeded in heading off U.S. government meddling in Mexican affairs, the publicity and opposition they stirred up could not totally be ignored.[3]

The PLM desperately needed to become prominently involved in revolutionary activity within Mexico. With few resources other than the public's positive association of Flores Magón with anti-Díaz agitation, seizure of territory would be possible only on the extreme fringe of the Mexican republic. Thus, an armed attack on thinly populated Baja California made sense. Ricardo's contacts and influence among Southern Californian radicals could compensate for material weakness and provide additional manpower. To wait any longer risked conceding everything to Madero. Flores Magón, sensing the rush of events, and keenly aware of Madero's growing popularity, felt the pressure of time.

Flores Magón's international view of Mexican affairs shaped the nature of the 1911 Baja California invasion, and explained the PLM's willingness to enlist non-Mexicans in the armed attack. In a manifesto directed at the International Workers of the World, the PLM stressed that the struggle went beyond Mexico, indeed it was a fight between social classes which would soon have as "its stage the surface of the whole planet, and was designed to smash tyranny, capitalism, and authority."[4] Unfortunately, foreign participation in the Baja campaign tinged the whole episode with undertones of filibusterism, which continue to distort modern interpretations of the incident.

The general plan called for the establishment of a PLM base within Mexico conveniently close to the border to facilitate logistics and if necessary, ready access to sanctuary in the United States. From Baja California the social revolution could be spread across the northern tier of states and then into central Mexico. With luck, spontaneous outbreaks might quicken the pace of revolution. Arms and ammunition gathered by John Kenneth Turner and the IWW in Chicago had been smuggled into Mexico. A small PLM force seized Mexicali on January 29, 1911, and subsequently the villages of Algodones and Tecate. Tijuana fell to a group of Wobblies (Workers for IWW) only marginally under Flores Magón's control. Led by Rhys Pryce, a Welshman, it included only a few Mexicans. The fall of Tijuana represented the high point of the campaign. It immediately was overshadowed by a major victory for the Maderistas. One day after the PLM had taken Tijuana, Pascual Orozco's troops seized Ciudad Juárez in the name of Francisco Madero. Ironically, Madero had ordered him not to risk it for fear of provoking American intervention. The fall of the major border city across from El Paso, Texas, made the capture of Tijuana the day before pale into insignificance. As a result of the Orozco victory an agreement between the Díaz regime and Madero provided for the strongman's resignation, the appointment of a provisional government and elections. Porfirio Díaz resigned on May 25, 1911, and left the country. Madero's move to the presidential palace had become unstoppable.

Meanwhile the PLM's armed campaign began to take on comic opera aspects. As a result of its colorful participants, the whole episode could be turned into an amusing newspaper event. The opportunism of publicist Dick Ferris, and his proclamation of the whimsical and short-lived Republic of Baja California, added to the confusion concerning the nature of the invasion. Pryce ran off with the available cash. At its worst, newspaper coverage of events in Baja California made the PLM and Ricardo Flores Magón appear ridiculous, and at best incompetent. More seriously, it forced his socialist allies to examine their own position and attitude toward the Madero regime and their previously uncritical support of the PLM.[5]

The American Left's attitude toward the Madero government was ambivalent and confused. Much of their support had been anti-Díaz, rather than pro-Flores Magón; consequently, they viewed the Mexican revolution differently from the PLM. The revolution's continuing nature conflicted with their desire to see the establishment of a bourgeois capitalist democracy that could provide the future basis for a socialist state or, in the case of Samuel Gompers, recognition of labor's position within society. Thus, reaction to the PLM's call for continued struggle against Díaz's successor, Francisco Madero, was lukewarm at best. Mother Jones, who along with Frank Hayes, vice president of the UMW and Joseph Cannon of the WFM went to Mexico to confer with the new government, developed a favorable opinion of Francisco Madero. The fluidity of the sociopolitical climate in Mexico following Díaz's resignation convinced Mother Jones that a new age had dawned. In a telegram to the *Appeal to Reason* from Mexico City she announced that interim President Francisco León de la Barra had given her the right to organize Mexican miners. She boasted that such a privilege had never before been conceded in the history of Mexico and moreover it represented "the greatest concession ever granted anyone representing the laboring class of any nation." She claimed that President-elect Madero concurred and consequently she was the first person ever permitted to carry the "banner of industrial freedom to the . . . peons of this nation." Her total ignorance of Mexico's labor history and her naive and egotistical reaction to the vague promises of desperate revolutionary politicians must have stunned Flores Magón. At the request of the Mexican government she attempted to arrange a reconciliation between the Madero regime and the PLM. Ricardo's hostile reception of this information shocked and alienated her. She declared the PLM and its leadership to be a group of "unreasonable fanatics" of questionable honesty. According to her, Job Harriman and William B. Cleary also shared her disenchantment.[6] The *Appeal*, nevertheless, noted that Madero, as a member of the favored class, could not be expected to do more than establish capitalism in Mexico, yet that in itself constituted an advance beyond Díaz's feudalism.[7] In spite of doubts, the *Appeal* concluded that Madero was "doubtless a true patriot" worthy of support in the interests of ridding the country of an oppressive regime.[8] Less generously, the *New York Call* labeled Madero a tool of American business, a conclusion Flores Magón must have found heartening. Support for PLM activities in Baja, however, did not automatically follow from the paper's hostile assessment of Madero.[9]

The *Call* attacked the PLM anarchistic leadership, and ridiculed Ricardo Flores Magón's failure to personally lead the armed invasion of Baja California.[10] In Los Angeles, a group of socialists, in a face-to-face confrontation, demanded a clear statement of Flores Magón's personal political views.[11] Ricardo, however, hesitated to sacrifice any support and evaded a direct response. Such political vagueness appears to have been successful in holding on to some socialist support. W. G. Ghent, Wisconsin socialist Congressman Victor Berger's secretary, charged that some socialists had adopted a degree of "sentimental anarchism" leading them to forget that anarchism is as opposed to socialism as it is to capitalism. Contemptuously, he dismissed the invasion as "no more a class war . . . [than] a dozen hobos intent upon starting a roughhouse."[12]

Perhaps even more cuttingly, the *New York Call*, following Flores Magón's indictment, published an open letter from his former friend and colleague, Juan Sarabia, that accused Ricardo of attempting to force the Mexican people into anarchism against their will. Unkindly, Sarabia suggested that

Flores Magón's revolution violated natural law, and chided him for ignoring education, "the work of the brain not the brawn, of doctrines, not rifles."[13] To Ricardo Flores Magón, the intellectual, such criticism must have been insulting.

Anarchist Emma Goldman bitterly accused socialists of ignoring the most significant social uprising since the Paris Commune, and, in fact, of working with Wall Street, Washington, and Madero against the true Mexican revolution. Going even further, Goldman claimed that should the PLM be defeated, a large part of the blame would fall on the Socialist Party of America.[14]

Unexpected criticism came from the influential French anarchist journal, *Le Temps Nouveaux*, which berated Flores Magón for conducting his military campaign under the 1906 liberal program as well as for failing to play an active, personal part in the PLM's own armed struggle in Baja California. Perhaps the most destructive accusation made by the French journal was that Flores Magón used financial contributions merely to foment factionalism.[15] *Le Temps Nouveaux*, somewhat unwittingly, put its editorial finger on Flores Magón's major mistake—his failure to openly proclaim his anarchism proved to be a fatal error. The PLM already had lost its leadership role within Mexico and was never to recover it.

The collapse of the Baja invasion together with withering attacks from virtually all sides finally forced Ricardo to identify himself publicly as an anarchist. The PLM's new program, appropriately addressed "To the Workers of the World" and issued in September 1911, replaced the politically outdated 1906 platform. *Tierra y Libertad*, the anarchist slogan, now officially represented the PLM's sociopolitical goals.[16] In view of the harsh comments coming from every quarter, Ricardo gratefully welcomed kind words from Peter Kropotkin, one of the most influential international anarchists, who observed that anarchism constituted more than fighting at the barricades.[17] Kropotkin accepted William C. Owens's argument that Flores Magón, as an intellectual concerned with the movement's overall direction, could not be expected to participate in every phase of the revolution.[18] Anarchist ambivalence about the use of physical violence tended to make them less ready to condemn Ricardo Flores Magón's lack of personal participation in the actual attack. To many, violence represented a last resort. While the "propaganda of the deed" might be understandable as well as individually inspiring, it did not change the broad situation. Use of violence was a personal decision, not a philosophical imperative. Intellectual methods of moving toward anarchist objectives received greater attention. The movements major leaders spent their time lecturing, writing, and attempting to expand the philosophical perspective of their potential constituency. Respect for learning, an important part of the immigrant mystique, reinforced the tendency. Emma Goldman, Alexander Berkman, and Voltairine de Cleyre, as intellectuals, understood and appreciated Ricardo's similar orientation. At the same time many anarchists found individual acts of violence such as Berkman's physical attack on Henry C. Frick, president of the Carnegie Company and a prominent symbol of oppression, commendable. Nevertheless, they understood that the attempted murder of Frick had alienated public opinion and doomed the strike at the company's Homestead works to failure. Moreover, Berkman's act and subsequent years in prison had removed him from the active struggle. Thus, to many it appeared that the socialists used Flores Magón's lack of physical involvement in the Baja California campaign as a pretext to withdraw support.[19]

From a practical standpoint, lack of official socialist support placed Flores Magón in a difficult position, especially after his arrest. He could not afford to attack the party directly because of the important support of individual socialists, but at the same time, he had to defend himself and the PLM's activities. Fortunately, Emma Goldman's *Mother Earth* provided a vital forum for the PLM. In a letter published in *Mother Earth*, Flores Magón declared that the PLM was involved in a life-and-death struggle with capitalism, Francisco

Madero, and certain socialist leaders. The labor movement, as well as the socialists, must understand that the fight was vital and international in scope, consequently, "we of Los Angeles" should not carry the whole burden.[20] Any direct assault on the official socialist position could be left to Goldman or English anarchist William C. Owen, but it was not a luxury Flores Magón could afford to indulge.[21] In spite of the PLM's cautious attitude, socialist and trade-union support would be weakened by the struggle with Francisco Madero. Socialist Ethel Duffy Turner, wife of the author of *Barbarous Mexico*, resigned as *Regeneración*'s English language editor, although she continued personally to sympathize with Ricardo Flores Magón. Owen assumed her duties on the newspaper's editorial board.

Flores Magón believed that Madero could count on American support and sympathy to suppress the PLM. During the PLM's Baja California campaign American civil and military officials went beyond strict enforcement of the neutrality laws to harass and prevent the purchase of supplies and foodstuffs by the rebels. The United States government preferred to side with more traditional regimes, first that of Díaz then Madero, but not with what appeared to be a disorderly group of radicals, many fresh from hobo camps on the American side of the border. In fact, while Mexican officials had access to their American counterparts, they could not count on immediate or total cooperation. Nevertheless, because federal officers shared the Mexican government's antipathy toward anarchists they could be persuaded to take at least some action. Francisco León de la Barra, while Mexican Ambassador in Washington, repeatedly had urged Attorney General Wickersham to suppress *Regeneración*, and complained to Secretary of State Philander C. Knox about the activities of the Los Angeles group.[22] To support their charges, Mexican agents in California collected evidence against Flores Magón. Their findings subsequently became available to Madero. The June 1911 issue of *Mother Earth*, reflecting Ricardo's views, probably conveyed by Owen, described Madero as just another Díaz, even to the extent of employing the same "infamous and fiendish methods" to persecute the "Magonists of Lower California." With Emma Goldman's support, a Mexican Revolution Conference was organized in New York to support the PLM; and it scheduled a demonstration at the Cooper Union in the latter part of June. The Conference, under chairman Charles W. Lawson, dispatched a protest telegram to President Taft, and exchanged correspondence with Secretary of State Philander C. Knox about the transfer of Mexican political prisoners to Madero.[23] Such attempts to rally radical support against anticipated repression just barely preceded the arrest of the PLM's leadership.

If the socialists failed to develop a clear perception of the armed PLM's activities, Francisco Madero, however, did. In June 1911, he dispatched Ricardo's older brother, Jesús Flores Magón, and Juan Sarabia, the PLM's long-imprisoned and largely honorary vice-president, to negotiate a withdrawal and cooperation between them.[24] Madero had already indicated to federal officials that he favored Ricardo Flores Magón's arrest for violation of the neutrality laws.[25] Shortly after the failure of reconciliation attempts, Flores Magón and his brother Enrique, Librado Rivera, and several others were arrested, charged under the neutrality laws, and released on bail. Flores Magón deeply resented the delivery of Madero's message by his own brother, and bitterly blamed Francisco Madero for his subsequent arrest. In fact, the Justice Department already had decided the Los Angeles group included dangerous anarchists seeking to overthrow all established governments, including that of the United States, and their apprehension was desirable in the interests of internal security.[26]

In two separate indictments, both dated July 8, 1911, the grand jury listed seven counts of conspiracy to "hire and retain persons in the United States to enter service of foreign people as soldiers." The first indictment concerned the alleged enlistment of two Americans, and the second, of Mexican residents.[27] Defense lawyer Job Harriman subsequently challenged the court's jurisdiction, the manner in which the indictments had been drawn up, and the combining of separate counts in the two indictments.[28] This legal sparring could not avoid a trial, but did delay it until June of 1912. The *Los Angeles Times* attributed the delay to the efforts of Jesús Flores Magón, now secretary of government (internal security) in the Madero cabinet, who allegedly hoped the rift could be healed and, with pressure from the Mexican government, that only a nominal sentence would be imposed.[29]

The Madero regime, however, as a result of the unsuccessful reconciliation attempt, shared the United States government's desire to imprison Flores Magón, and thus eliminate the disruptive potential of the PLM leader. If he could not be co-opted, then he must be removed from politics. To ensure the desired end, the Mexican government hired Frank Stewart to represent its interests. Formerly an assistant United States attorney in the Los Angeles office, Stewart had interviewed witnesses and had been responsible for presenting the government's case to the grand jury to secure the original indictment of the PLM leaders. Well acquainted with all aspects of the case, and possessing excellent contacts within the judicial bureaucracy, he could be relied upon to ensure Mexican cooperation with the American authorities. In fact, Assistant Attorney General A. I. McCormick asked that Stewart be appointed a special assistant without pay so that he could officially participate in the prosecution.[30] The attorney general, however, declined but informed McCormick that Stewart could still be recognized, and through the device of professional courtesy, be permitted to assist in the government's case against the men.[31]

Emma Goldman attempted to build support for the PLM by sending copies of the "Manifesto to the Workers of the World" and *Regeneración*, along with an appeal for defense funds, to sympathizers around the world. In Australia, supporters distributed copies to the Trades Hall Council and the Socialist Party. From Portugal came $95 collected by the anarchist journal, *A Lanterna* of São Paulo, Brazil; the money was conveyed through Neno Vasco, the foremost Portuguese anarchist writer.[32] In Chicago, the Mexican Liberal Defense League, not content with lecturing to an IWW local and the Scandinavian Liberty League, distributed propaganda in England. Honoré Jaxon, the league's secretary, arranged to have a statement concerning the Mexican revolution printed up and distributed by the Standing Orders Committee of the British Trade Unions, and managed to have interviews published in the Manchester *Labour Leader* as well as in other journals. Returning to Chicago by way of Canada, Jaxon lectured before trade union groups in Montreal, Quebec, and Toronto, in addition to publishing interviews in those cities.[33] An impressive number of petitions, telegrams, and printed *coupones de protestas* arrived at the White House and the Department of Justice; some demanded the release of the men, and others insisted they be given sufficient time to call favorable witnesses. Most, but not all, of the signatures were of Mexican and Mexican-American PLM supporters.[34]

In spite of such efforts, the political climate could hardly have been less propitious for the defendants. Socialism, joined with radicalism in the public mind, reached a high point of activity in the state in 1911; and the following year, the forces of reaction were in command. General Harrison Gray Otis, owner and editor of the *Los Angeles Times*, led the charge. The *Times*, in the name of industrial liberty, but in the interests of the Merchants and Manufacturer's Association, fought against the union shop.[35] After the dynamiting of the *Times* building in 1910, General Otis declared all-out war on the Left. Initially, he attacked the union movement, but soon broadened his campaign to encompass the entire left-wing spectrum. There was even speculation that the PLM played a role in the *Times* bombing. In Los Angeles, the Mexican Consul, Antonio Lozano, wrote Foreign Affairs Minister Federico Gamboa that some believed Ricardo Flores Magón to be involved.[36] The fact that socialist lawyer Job Harriman had forged a political alliance with union labor made it easier to issue blanket condemnations. The AFL and the socialists defended unionism against the charges leveled by the *Times*, while the IWW called for a general strike to protect the innocent from the "relentless vengeance of capitalism."[37] Unfortunately, the public equated working-class militancy with extremism.[38]

Emma Goldman, lecturing on the West Coast, found California "seething with discontent."[39] The arrest of the McNamara brothers in connection with the *Times* explosion and their erroneous identification as anarchists, instead of the trade unionists they were; armed PLM activities in Baja California which attracted the support of anarchists, Wobblies, socialists, and other assorted elements; Job Harriman's mayoral campaign; and the editorial hysteria of the *Los Angeles Times* all combined to heighten the tension in Southern California.

Subsequently, the guilty pleas of the suspected dynamiters in December of 1911 brought down the socialist-trade union alliance and destroyed Harriman's hope of capturing the office of Los Angeles mayor. Hostility toward the Left was kept alive by such events as the free-speech struggles of the IWW. In San Diego, a massive demonstration in 1912 involved several thousand participants and was only broken up by the use of firehoses. A local paper suggested the demonstrators be shot or hanged.[40] 1912 could not be considered a favorable one for a suspected anarchist, associated with the IWW and the socialists, to come to trial. The fact that the state and society felt beleaguered by political violence led to a disregard for justice in the interest of crushing what appeared to be the possibility of class warfare. By the time Flores Magón appeared before the court, most of the related cases growing out of the PLM's invasion of Baja California had been resolved. The government now moved to deal directly with the movement's leaders. Willedd Andrews replaced Job Harriman as the group's attorney before the trial began on June 4, 1912.[41]

Because of the political climate, the government conducted the trial more to satisfy the desire to control extremism than to uphold neutrality laws. The issue of the Baja invasion became the vehicle by which anarchists could be imprisoned. The association of Flores Magón with extremism would be reinforced in the public's mind by the presence in the courtroom itself of extremely vocal women supporters who wore red banners printed with the anarchists' slogan across their breasts, while male supporters loudly proclaimed themselves anarchists and insulted the American flag. A *Times* reporter noted that a man named Webster, to show his contempt for authority, took out a knife and began carving on the wainscotting.[42] Webster may have been a member of the IWW group in attendance.[43] Dudley W. Robinson, the assistant United States attorney, recalled that every morning the courtroom seemed to be packed with a solid phalanx of red. As the trial progressed, Robinson claimed to have recognized IWW members who had taken part in the San Diego riot as well as part of the gang allegedly involved in a plot to blow up the Los Angeles Hall of Records. Flores Magón's supporters obviously managed to impress the prosecution, even if they failed to influence the trial's outcome.[44]

The government, undeterred by the lack of witnesses, resorted to fabrication. Peter Martin, subsequently detained on suspicion of offering a child poisoned candy, and Paul Schmidt, a smuggler who later claimed that the government promised him immunity, served, among others, as witnesses.[45] Under cross-examination, Martin admitted spying on Flores Magón for the Mexican government; in effect, he testified as a paid witness.[46] Defense witnesses could not be as easily produced; indeed, Quirino Lemón, described by the *Times* as a "specimen Mexican outlaw," was arrested in the courtroom before he could testify.[47]

Attorney Willedd Andrews failed to get the judge to agree to bring in witnesses from outside the district at government expense. The prosecutor entered copies of *Regeneración*, numerous letters, and copies of commissions as evidence. Andrews argued that the PLM had not violated the neutrality laws. Apparently in an effort to provide another target, as well as an explanation of border events, the defense stated that John D. Spreckels, a well-known industrialist, had financed the campaign. Such a contention not only discredited the PLM's ideals, but also could not be taken seriously. It may have been possible to believe that Spreckels became involved to protect his own interests, but certainly not in support of Flores Magón. In any event, Judge Wellborn reminded the court that the proceedings concerned the matter of violation of the neutrality laws, not whether others had financed the PLM.[48] A conspiracy charge could be sustained without difficulty. In its final summation, the government pointed out that the charge alleged conspiracy, not the actual enlistment of soldiers, therefore, even if the defendents did not actually hire anyone, they could still be found guilty. Moreover, actual success or failure did not enter into consideration because the thing made punishable was the "unlawful meeting of the minds." The drawing of rational conclusions based on circumstantial evidence would be the jury's task. The prosecution cautioned the jury to avoid decisions based on private political opinions, an obvious impossibility given the times.[49]

Andrews, in the defense's closing arguments, attempted to construct a strict definition of conspiracy, reminding the jury to disregard testimony they believed to be malicious. Andrews carefully implied that government witnesses were not impartial, and, in fact, had been instructed by the government.[50] The futility of the defense's efforts was underscored by the judge's instructions, which paralleled those of the government.[51]

Rather surprisingly, the jury deliberated until after midnight before reaching a decision. The next day, on June 22, 1912, the jury returned a verdict finding Ricardo Flores Magón, Enrique Flores Magón, and Librado Rivera guilty of three counts and Anselmo L. Figueroa of two counts of conspiracy. Hostile reactions from courtroom spectators caused the authorities to remove the convicted men hurriedly to the county jail. As news of the verdict spread, a number of individuals, shouting "down with the United States and President Taft," demonstrated both in front of the jail and the federal court building. A man, reported by the *Times* to be connected with the IWW, urged the crowd to demand entrance to the jail. Meanwhile, Lucille Norman Guidera, Ricardo's stepdaughter, allegedly entered the jail and assaulted the jailer. The *Los Angeles Times* headlined their report "IWW and Anarchy."[52]

On June 25, the men again appeared before the court for sentencing. The government requested a severe exemplary sentence, declaring that the PLM had previously been involved in other violations of the law, and could be expected to continue unless discouraged by the court. Andrews, on the other hand, pointed out that the conspiracy charge had only barely been sustained; therefore, the judge should not impose a harsh prison term. Judge Wellborn compromised by pronouncing a sentence of one year and eleven months in the federal penitentiary at McNeil Island, Washington.[53]

Immediately following the sentencing, heavily armed guards returning the men to county jail were followed by a group of supporters led by Lucille Norman. The crowd, estimated at 2,000 by nervous police observers, forcefully resisted attempts to disperse them. More than 100 policemen armed with clubs and guns battled them for more than an hour. Seventeen individuals, including Ricardo's stepdaughter, were arrested and a number injured.[54] Subsequently, officials charged there had been a plot to free the men. To avoid similar incidents, the men were removed from their cells on the evening of July 4, and spirited aboard a train to McNeil Island to begin serving their terms.[55]

In Los Angeles, PLM supporters began circulating petitions calling for overturning the conviction on the grounds that the government had resorted to perjured testimony. A series of affidavits subsequently published in *Regeneración* supported such claims. In spite of such protests, the government refused to reopen the case, thus tempting Emma Goldman to speculate that the officials hoped to curry favor with powerful interests on both sides of the border.[56] A group of supporters approached Congressman John P. Nolan to press for a pardon, and appealed to President Woodrow Wilson to examine the proceedings and pardon the prisoners. The President, supposedly after close study, denied clemency.[57]

4

"Let the Court Speak!
History Watches!"
Los Angeles, 1916

McNeil Island's Mexican prisoners marked time as others struggled to keep the PLM alive in Los Angeles. William C. Owen, fellow anarchist and editor of *Regeneración*'s English-language page, Blas Lara, and Teodoro Gaytán published the newspaper intermittently during the enforced absence of its regular staff. Editorials constantly reminded readers of the plight of the "Martyrs of McNeil," encouraging them to send their protests directly to President Taft and, later, to President Woodrow Wilson. In the columns of her paper, Emma Goldman kept the Flores Magón imprisonment before the radical community. Wealthy socialist entrepreneur and editor of *Wilshire's Magazine*, Gaylord Wilshire, noting that George Bernard Shaw had refused to lecture in the United States because of the country's propensity to throw its best citizens in jail, observed to his readers that the Mexican patriots, Flores Magón and Rivera, served as good cases in point.[1] In Tacoma, Washington, the editors of the radical newspaper *Why* visited the men at McNeil Island, reporting that they remained full of revolutionary purpose, and indeed an inspiration for others to follow; men who unselfishly offered their lives to the cause of human emancipation only to become "prisoners of the class war."[2]

The overall political climate in the country continued to deteriorate, particularly in California. In August 1913, a violent agricultural protest erupted in Wheatland. E. B. Durst, owner of a major hop farm and the largest single employer of agricultural labor in California, purposely attracted surplus migrant workers so he could drive down the already low wages of agricultural labor. Faced with inadequate housing, insufficient water, little or no sanitation, and dependent on Durst's own store for food, more than 3,000 persons, including many Mexican as well as other nationalities, revolted. While IWW activists had attempted to organize resistance, the uprising was a spontaneous reaction to exploitation. Governor Hiram Johnson dispatched National Guard troops to maintain order while the owners responded by organizing the Farmer's Protective League to discourage future labor uprisings. Two IWW organizers received life sentences on trumped-up second-degree murder charges.[3]

Meanwhile, in Los Angeles, Mexican radicals regrouped, establishing the *Casa del Obrero Internacional,* headed by the founder of the Mexican *Casa del Obrero Mundial* in Mexico City, Juan Francisco Moncaleano. A Colombian anarchist and political fugitive, Moncaleano arrived in Mexico in 1912. As a former university professor, he believed the masses must be educated along the lines advocated by the Catalan anarchist, Francisco Ferrer Guardia. Worker schools free of government influence would supply the tools necessary to liberate the mind. Moncaleano, an admirer and fervent supporter of Ricardo Flores Magón, used his short-lived newspaper *Luz* to publicize the PLM's program.[4] He arrived in Los Angeles after his expulsion from Mexico on the eve of the opening of the *Casa del Obrero Mundial* in Mexico City. The Los Angeles *Casa* was headquartered in a former orphanage. *Regeneración* announced the new organization belonged to all workers of the world, who could depend both on moral and material support in the form of dormitory and bathing facilities, medical aid, and food for the body as well as the mind.[5] By contrast, the *Los Angeles Times* reported that the old orphanage would be used to train troops, supposedly under the direction of the imprisoned leaders, mysteriously employing Yaqui Indian runners to carry messages between Los Angeles and McNeil Island.[6] Such flights of fancy occasioned bitter amusement among the ranks of the PLM.

Finally, early in the morning of January 19, 1914, their twenty-three-month sentences shortened by four months for good behavior, Ricardo and Enrique Flores Magón, Librado Rivera, and Anselmo Figueroa walked out of McNeil Island Federal Penitentiary. On hand to greet them was William C. Owen, who had left Los Angeles earlier on a speaking tour, arriving in the Pacific Northwest shortly before their release. Together with various labor, socialist, and radical groups, Owen organized a series of mass meetings at which the released men appeared. On the evening of their release, the former prisoners attended a reception in Tacoma, followed by other appearances in Seattle, Portland, and San Francisco on their way back to Southern California.[7]

These meetings, besides honoring the ex-prisoners and celebrating their freedom, served as fund-raisers for the continuation of the political struggle. Despite poor economic conditions and widespread unemployment in the Northwest, the Portland meeting, presided over by Dr. C. H. Chapman, editorial writer of the *Oregonian*, netted them $46.22, while the Seattle gathering, where hundreds of IWW members reportedly marched in procession to the local labor temple meeting, brought in slightly more.[8] Such donations, seemingly pitifully small, were important to men who lived a hand-to-mouth existence in order to sustain their efforts. The desperation with which they clung to the newspaper was poignantly underscored by Enrique's wife, who accused him of putting the welfare of the PLM before that of his wife and children.[9] Certainly, the continued publication of the newspaper became the political as well as emotional reason for their existence, and they willingly sacrificed their own physical well-being to keep it alive and before the public. *Regeneración*'s publication remained the major pretext for continued harassment by federal authorities and local officials.

Within a week of their release, the Flores Magóns were back in Los Angeles, ready to go to work. A short piece, bordered on the front page of the January 31, 1914, issue of *Regeneración* and titled "Once Again in Our Place," announced their return.[10] Despite various problems, especially financial, they expressed their hope to put the paper back on its feet, concluding, characteristically, "now to work with the same determination as before, until death or victory."[11]

During their year-and-a-half at McNeil Island, momentous changes had swept Mexico. President Francisco Madero, overthrown by General Victoriano Huerta in February 1913, died at the hands of the new regime. Widespread opposition arose quickly throughout the republic, and fighting broke out against Huerta and his federal army. Francisco Villa, Emiliano Zapata, and the governor of the State of Coahuila, Venustiano Carranza, emerged as leaders of the various opposition forces, only loosely bound together against the Huerta government. The factionalism that characterized the opposition had the effect of splintering the followers of the PLM, both in Mexico and the United States who still looked to Ricardo Flores Magón for leadership. Most of them gradually aligned themselves with one or another of the various opposition leaders. In order to re-establish some ideological control, Flores Magón, just a little over a month after his release, analyzed the Mexican revolution in a major speech subsequently published on the front page of *Regeneración* under the heading, "Orientation of the Mexican Revolution." Firmly insisting that it must be viewed as a social revolution, not one of individuals, he characterized such politicians as "Villa, Carranza, Vázquez Gómez, and Félix Díaz as mere froth thrown up by the social agitation to be skimmed off, making room for successive layers until the skimming process resulted in the removal of all impurities."[12]

The PLM not only had to curb the defection of its own followers, but also sought to convince American supporters not to back the Constitutionalists and their self-appointed chief Venustiano Carranza. Anarchists such as Emma Goldman and Alexander Berkman did not need to be warned against Carranza, because philosophically they opposed the creation of a state and saw the essential continuity of the struggle in the demands of the peasantry for land. Others, however, believed that the fall of an individual president was politically important. Anarchist intellectual Voltairine de Cleyre, in a lecture delivered in Chicago shortly after the imprisonment of Flores Magón, correctly emphasized the difficulty of convincing the Left that victory over one government did not mean the end of the Mexican revolution. The socialists, with their reports of a "new" revolution, totally failed to comprehend that the substitution of one "political manager" for another did not resolve the basic economic questions.[13]

Voltairine de Cleyre became the Chicago correspondent of *Regeneración* and along with Honoré Jaxon organized the Mexican Liberal Defense League and served as its treasurer. Using her influence among Chicago radicals she raised funds for the PLM at mass meetings and picnics. In a series of lectures she pleaded for support for Flores Magón and the remnants of his organization. Joseph Kucera, in collaboration with de Cleyre, wrote an article on the Mexican revolution for the New York Czech press. De Cleyre hoped to move to Los Angeles and join the struggle. Unfortunately, failing health made that impossible and Kucera went in her place. Her last effort on behalf of the PLM was a poem titled "Written-in-Red" that appeared in *Regeneración* six months before her death.[14]

To Flores Magón's anarchist supporters, Mexican revolutionary violence appeared to be part of the worldwide "economic revolution" bursting out in one area, only to be stiffled, then breaking out elsewhere—now Mexico, next London, then Paris or Chicago.[15] The various elements of the Left, on the other hand, found it difficult to accept the call for continued struggle. PLM hostility, first toward Francisco Madero, then Venustiano Carranza, seemed to many an indication of political jealousy as well as a lack of solidarity. Carranza's willingness to cooperate with the anarchistically inclined *Casa del Obrero Mundial* seemed to be positive proof of his working-class sympathies. The organization of worker's battalions to assist in the campaign to retake Mexico City from the Villistas and Zapatistas, in exchange for government support of working-class objectives, appealed to the Left.

Samuel Gompers of the AFL, a valuable ally of Flores

Magón during the anti-Díaz period, now saw cooperation with Carranza, in the interests of the worker, as the most promising and fruitful course. Ironically, John Murray, who had expressed support for Ricardo previously, became Gompers's chief adviser on Mexican affairs. Murray also served as a government informant on radical labor movements and undoubtedly played a role in the molding of official policy toward the various factions in the Mexican revolutionary struggle.[16] Long involved in organizing Mexican-American workers in Los Angeles, Murray first met Ricardo through his friend Job Harriman, and in 1908 made a trip to Mexico with credentials supplied by the PLM. Murray suggested that the AFL establish formal ties with Mexican labor, smoothing over objections that the *Casa del Obrero Mundial* appeared too radical by explaining that its radicalism stemmed from Spanish roots. The projected alliance between the *Casa* and the AFL necessitated Gompers's support for United States recognition of the Carranza regime. Consequently, Gompers wrote to President Wilson, stating that he believed Carranza to be a friend of the Mexican worker as well as a true representative of Mexican democracy. In fact, Gompers's objectives in Mexico had diverged sharply from those of Flores Magón. Subsequently, the establishment of the Pan American Federation of Labor (1918), designed to be a Latin American version of the AFL, symbolized the fundamental incompatibility of their positions.[17]

Gompers, while privately harboring reservations, nevertheless publicly placed himself squarely behind Carranza. In the same fashion, the socialists had more in common with the Mexican government than with the anarchist leadership of the PLM, who, in fact, appeared to be increasingly out of touch with the political realities of post-Díaz Mexico. Subsequently, John Kenneth Turner, author of *Barbarous Mexico* and an old associate of Flores Magón, considered Carranza's consolidation of power a victory for socialism and organized labor.[18] The political fortunes of the Flores Magóns and their core of followers had already peaked and were in decline, a fact sensed by many elements of the Left. One could admire them as revolutionaries, worthy of respect and sympathy perhaps, but hardly as the center of political action. In fact, Flores Magón correctly perceived Carranza's opportunistic labor policy. Barely six months after receiving American recognition, labor circles would be shocked by the implementation of a decree, based on an 1862 statute, that made it treason to strike against the government's interests. From that point on, socialist and AFL support for Carranza would be a bit more ambivalent, yet not sufficiently so to guarantee the PLM more than limited support.[19] Carranza's antistrike decree, however, was a cause for jubilation among the PLM leadership in Los Angeles. Enrique Flores Magón wrote a long letter to Emma Goldman for publication in *Mother Earth*, analyzing the labor policy of the Mexican government. In his letter, Enrique emphasized that Carranza, like every shrewd politician, talked and acted as a radical only when he needed labor-class support. The "Red Battalions," which included socialists as well as anarchists of the *Casa del Obrero Mundial*, had been duped. Enrique observed that he knew many radicals, and even anarchists, who supported the Carranza government, and some even advised the PLM to work with that regime to educate them in the ideals of communist-anarchism—a position Enrique found "so funny."[20]

Taking advantage of the propaganda opportunity created by the antistrike legislation, the PLM issued a manifesto "To the Workers of the United States."[21] Not intended to be a ringing declaration, but rather a reasoned plea for working-class support, the manifesto noted that both President Woodrow Wilson and the PLM agreed that the primary cause of the Mexican revolution was economic—in particular, the agrarian problem. Given such high-level agreement, the PLM called on all class-conscious workers to lend the Los Angeles group their moral and material support; "after all, the cause of the wage-slave against his master has no frontier." The manifesto urged its intended audience to think in terms of a universal struggle against hunger and poverty. In case the American worker failed to grasp the importance of the Mexican revolution, the PLM noted that the flood of Mexican immigrants into the Southwest and beyond, to mine and till the land from California, Texas, and Illinois, directly affected the livelihood of the American worker. Unless Mexican labor received economic justice in its own land, it would depress the wage level in the United States.

Looking even further ahead, the PLM's leadership warned that eventually American industrialists would transfer their operations south of the border to exploit cheap Mexican labor, leaving closed-down factories in the north. The document called for international solidarity, since what affected labor in one country had an impact on labor in all others. In an effort to counter doubts about the honesty of the PLM leadership expressed following the Baja invasion, the manifesto declared that the "best guarantee of our honesty is the twenty-two years that we have undergone in dungeons where tyranny would thrust its fangs in our throat to punish our loyalty and devotion to the interests of the working class." Moreover, the personal poverty of the leadership also offered proof of their refusal to ignore their conscience or betray the high ideals of the PLM.[22] Significantly, no mention was made of the party's anarchism; and in fact, the arguments set forth were so broad that the IWW and craft unionists could agree in principle.

Such propaganda efforts probably had little impact. As long as Ricardo Flores Magón avoided political alliances with active revolutionaries and remained in Los Angeles, the impression that the PLM was far removed from the real action persisted.[23] In Mexico, political power combinations changed with bewildering speed, creating at least an illusion of change, while in California the Flores Magóns and *Regeneración* continued, as always, a marginal existence.

Ricardo had a number of opportunities to ally himself with active revolutionary groups. Emiliano Zapata, in particular, was receptive to PLM influence. His Plan of Ayala (November 11, 1911) reflected concepts from Flores Magón's manifesto of September 1911, and incorporated phrases drawn from the pages of *Regeneración*.[24] As early as 1912, Zapata proposed moving the PLM and its newspaper to Morelos. The Fabrica San Rafael, under Zapatista control, could supply all the necessary newsprint, while Zapata's armed followers guaranteed freedom of operation. Ricardo, already enmeshed in the American judicial machinery, was in no position to return to Mexico; so Zapata's offers were declined.[25]

The PLM thus missed the opportunity to join a successful peasant and worker's movement that could have supplied the force to move Flores Magón's ideas out of theory and into action. Likewise, the PLM leader's hostility toward Pancho Villa was a major mistake. By choosing to view Villa as part of the "scum" thrown up by the revolution, Ricardo failed to grasp the fact that both of them identified with the dispossessed. The energy of the masses reached a high point with the seizure of Mexico City by the Villistas and Zapatistas. If the PLM had chosen the admittedly difficult as well as dangerous role of active participant and philosophical guide in the popular movement, the occupation of the capital might well have been more than a futile demonstration.

Critics of Ricardo's reluctance to become directly and physically involved in revolutionary activity within Mexico were correct—it cost him his leadership influence. American authorities now took Flores Magón more seriously than the great bulk of former PLM members who had joined in support of the active participants in the Mexican revolution. William C. Owen subsequently recalled that Flores Magón opposed transferring the paper to Mexico because he believed that *Regeneración* had the special mission of building up sentiment in the United States against an armed intervention in Mexican affairs.[26]

In 1915, public attention focused dramatically on Mexican-American activities in the Southwest with the sudden increase of border violence, as well as the discovery of the Plan of San Diego. Allegedly drawn up in January of that year in San Diego, Texas, but signed in the Monterrey prison, the plan called for a general uprising on February 20, 1915, with the goal of seizing the territory that had been taken from

Mexico between 1836 and 1848. The reconquered territory would then become a separate republic, and perhaps eventually be reannexed to Mexico—in effect an exact reversal of the process by which the United States acquired Texas. The plan specifically named the territorial objectives as Texas, New Mexico, Arizona, Colorado, and Upper California. Racial as well as class tensions could easily be distinguished in the plan's clauses. Other oppressed groups, including "Indians, Negroes, and Orientals," were envisioned as allies who in turn might also be rewarded territorially, while every male American above the age of sixteen as well as Mexican traitors would be killed.[27] Just how many Mexican-American and Mexican residents responded to the Plan of San Diego is unknown; however, a number of serious skirmishes between U.S. cavalry patrols and alleged adherents occurred, and quasi-military units had been formed supposedly to implement the plan.[28] The threatened revolt was believable because of the well-recognized frustration and hatred engendered by social restrictions, as well as open discrimination against Mexican-Americans in Texas.

Frontier unrest, however, cannot be traced to a single source—the political situation itself was very complex. President Carranza clearly used border unrest to strengthen the case for recognition. Mexican diplomats emphasized that only a strong, recognized, and legitimate government could cooperate with the United States in restoring stability to the region. Border violence, interlaced with international political considerations, local prejudices, Mexican nationalism, irredentism as well as simple and social banditry, did, in fact, die down with the recognition of the Carranza regime and the development of cooperative measures against disorderly elements. Meanwhile, racial antagonism led to violence, vigilante tactics and arbitrary action by the Texas Rangers. Secret Service agent Edward Tyrell reported that in the vicinity of Brownsville over 300 Mexicans had been killed, many in "cold blood."[29] The population of the lower Rio Grande valley, fearing an invasion from Mexico and intimidated by the widespread random terrorism, thinned out as Anglos sent their families northward, while those of Mexican origin retreated to the safety of northern Mexico.

By late October 1915 the United States Army concentrated virtually half its mobile reserves along the border between Laredo and Brownsville. The necessity of such drastic action impressed both the army and the federal government with the dangerous potential of the unstable Mexican situation. Moreover, the natural equalitarian impulse of the revolution made Mexican Americans less willing to suffer the social and class prejudices considered normal in the Southwest. The pressure for change caused a predictable reaction against Mexicans. Taking adroit advantage of the situation, Carranza agents filed a complaint against Ricardo Flores Magón and his newspaper with the United States Postal Service. The complaint alleged that *Regeneración* incited border unrest and encouraged Mexican-American residents to resort to violence in their efforts to resist American authority. Such charges were calculated to disassociate the Carranza government with border violence, and at the same time, place the blame on the PLM. After the discovery of the Plan of San Diego, such suggestions seemed plausible to American officials.[30]

Although no evidence has been found showing a direct connection between the PLM and the Plan of San Diego, the link between the Los Angeles group and events in Texas appeared plausible in spite of the fact that by 1915 the PLM had lost much of its influence among border militants. Nevertheless, PLM followers had been arrested earlier—in September 1913—in connection with border raids, and they remained in jail throughout the difficult period.[31] *Regeneración* conducted a publicity campaign aimed at freeing the men, carefully tying in the PLM with the reaction against the social oppression in Texas. Flores Magón constantly demanded protection and justice for Mexican Americans against uncontrolled vigilantes and the Texas Rangers. Unfortunately, the PLM's efforts had a greater impact on the Justice Department than it had on the Texans. In Los Angeles, the *Times* could be counted on to keep a hostile watch over local PLM activities. Literal interpretations of Ricardo's rhetoric assured eye-catching, if distorted, stories. A meeting, held at the Silver Swan Hall on East Third Street in support of the junta and its leaders, was reported in terms suggestive of a dangerous conspiracy. According to the *Los Angeles Times*, a general uprising, seizure of the land, and an assault on local jails had been planned at the gathering. The "notorious Magón brothers," described as "ex-cons" aided by others of the same "anarchistic stripe," intended to begin a program of assassination, looting, and general terrorism. Reflecting fears about border violence and the Plan of San Diego, the paper reported that the PLM plan called for Mexican revolutionaries to seize California and Texas, then reannex them to Mexico as soon as war broke out between the two countries. The audience, described as "lower class Mexicans," including many women and children, sang what the reporter termed the "anarchistic Marseillaise," likened to a pianola suddenly gone mad and incoherent. The reporter, setting the tone of his article, noted that the "mescal tenor" and "perfumed soprano" each seemed to be singing something entirely different. More than likely, they sang new words composed by Enrique to reflect the PLM's beliefs, while many others in the crowd sang the Mexican national anthem in the traditional fashion.[32]

Enrique spoke first, followed by Blas Lara, who called for an uprising against the oppressive "gringo" along with the recapture of the land stolen from Mexico. Ricardo, in his typically fiery style, concluded with advice to use bombs and pistols as the only method to overthrow the capitalists. The *Los Angeles Times* failed to point out that the Silver Swan meeting coincided with the weekend-long Mexican Independence Day celebration, a time that might be expected to call for rallying the Mexican-American community; nevertheless, such rhetoric, placed in the context of the border unrest of that year, easily alarmed the general public. Noting that both the Flores Magón brothers appeared emaciated, the story concluded with the ominous remark that "a close watch is being kept upon them by the police and federal authorities and should their talk be taken too seriously, steps will be taken at once to return them to their resting place as guests of the government."[33]

Such steps had, in fact, already been taken. Ricardo, as early as November 1915, observed that Los Angeles postal authorities seemed to be preparing a case against the paper. He reported on a circular, dated November 4, 1915, sent by postal inspector Walter M. Cookson to *Regeneración* subscribers asking for copies of the September and October 1915 issues. Flores Magón charged postal authorities with violating constitutional guarantees of freedom of the press, as well as with demonstrating once again the farcical nature of American political liberties.[34]

Their fears of political retaliation were justified. On February 18, 1916, a grand jury indicted the Flores Magón brothers and William C. Owens on three counts of violating section 211 of the penal code of 1910.[35] Section 211 declared nonmailable material to be "obscene, lewd, or lascivious, and every filthy book, pamphlet, picture, paper, letter, writing, print or other publication of an indecent character." An amendment defined "indecent" as including material "tending to incite arson, murder, or assassination."[36] The first count charged the defendants with depositing copies of *Regeneración* containing "vile and filthy substance and language"; specifically, the paragraph that read:

> Wilson is in connivance with Carranza, because the old sharper has promised Wilson that he would favor American capitalists in Mexico. That is to say, Carranza has promised to deliver the Mexican people, tied hand and foot, to the same rapacious American plutocracy that had Díaz enslaved.

The second count cited a long excerpt that declared:

> Justice, and not bullets, is what ought to be given to the revolutionists of Texas, and from now on, one should demand that those persecutions of innocent Mexicans should cease and as to the revolutionists, we should also demand that they not be executed (shot). The ones who should be shot are the "rangers" and the band or bandits who accompany them in their depredations. Enough of reforms! What we hungry people need is entire liberty based on economic indepen-

dence. Down with the so-called rights of private property, and as long as this evil right continues to exist, we shall continue under arms. Enough with mockery! Poor people, whoever speaks to you about Carranzismo, spit in their face and break their jaw. Long live land and liberty!

A paragraph warning revolutionaries against surrendering their weapons "until you attain the triumph of the principles . . . that advocate the death of capital, of authority, and the clergy of all religions" constituted the basis for the third count. Flores Magón observed that politicians could not be effective, and that true liberty depended on land expropriation. Capitalists had to be dealt with in the same manner as "we get rid of the tiger, as we annihilate the rattlesnake, as we crush the tarantula." The indictment charged that such language fell within the definition of obscene nonmailable material contained in the penal code.[37]

Armed with handguns and sawed-off shotguns, deputy marshals, assisted by Los Angeles city police, descended on the Edendale headquarters to apprehend the indicted men. Owen, safely in Washington state, escaped arrest. Ricardo was quickly handcuffed and dragged from the building to a waiting police car. Enrique, however, challenged both the authority and motives of the officers; as a result of such boldness, he required a half-dozen stitches to close a head wound. Supporters, overwhelmed by the display of force, could only stand by in powerless frustration. With considerable satisfaction, the *Times* reported that the authorities held the "red brothers" on $7,500 bail.[38] Enrique questioned the large sum, implying, correctly, that the district attorney hoped to prevent its posting.

The government informed the court that one of the defendants had attacked a deputy during the arrest, while Enrique, still bearing the scars acquired during his apprehension, protested in vain. The defendants informed the court that they wished to consult with Job Harriman before deciding on their course of action. Harriman's ill health probably prevented his active participation in Flores Magón's defense. The *Los Angeles Examiner* reported that Harriman left the hospital around February 21; presumably, he had been hospitalized at the time of Flores Magón's arrest.[39] Subsequently, James H. Ryckman assumed direction of the defense, succeeding in obtaining a reduction of the bail to $5,000, in spite of strenuous prosecution objections that, if released, the defendants would disappear as had Owen.[40] Socialist attorney Ernest E. Kirk later joined Ryckman in the legal defense of the Flores Magóns.[41]

A telegram was sent to Emma Goldman in an effort to rally support for the jailed men. Subsequently, Ricardo's wife, María, wrote Goldman a long letter describing the circumstances of the arrest. María related that the police had used the nearby residence of a priest to stage their raid. When questioned, the officers indicated their belief that the reason for the arrest was a PLM conspiracy against the Carranza government.[42] Another letter went to Alexander Berkman in San Francisco, dramatically portraying the arrest as a siege, with a "swarm of bulls" leaping from the shrubbery pressing weapons into the ribs of anyone who made the slightest move to resist.[43] To Berkman, the arrest of the PLM's leadership formed part of a general pattern of suppression designed to eliminate disruptive elements in the face of impending war. The raid on the new anarchist monthly, the *Alarm*, the arrest of Emma Goldman in New York; and other threatening actions of the federal government appeared to fit in with the Flores Magón case—Wilson "the lackey of Carranza," tying up loose ends in the interest of capitalistic solidarity.[44] The *Blast*, Berkman's paper, urged a campaign of mass meetings and publicity to force the government to back down on both the Emma Goldman and Flores Magón cases. Alexander Berkman himself organized a mass meeting in San Francisco on March 8, 1916, to protest Flores Magón's arrest. Although it arrived too late, the brothers, from their cell in the county jail, wrote an appreciative letter to be read at the meeting blaming the "bandits of Wall Street" for their unhappy circumstances.[45]

From his sanctuary in Washington state, Owen attacked the postal monopoly as the government's most powerful weapon against radicals. Owen linked the arrests to the willingness of Carranza to cooperate with the United States in restoring order, protecting private property and indemnifying foreign speculators. *Regeneración's* editors opposed the Carranza regime because that government intended to restore every oppressive element associated with the Díaz regime; the United States, as Carranza's backer, had become just as interested in the suppression of the PLM as the Mexican government.[46] To Owen and Alexander Berkman the arrests signalled a return to the close cooperation that had existed along the frontier between federal officers and Mexican authorities during the Porfiriato. They could not have been aware of the deep antipathy existing between Woodrow Wilson and Carranza, which made cooperation a grudging affair.

In Los Angeles, supporters organized an International Workers Defense League in concert with similar groups around the country.[47] Envisioned as a permanent association of all those interested in the struggle for economic justice, including socialists, anarchists, single-taxers, the IWW, and "rebels without a label," the organization drew its members from every nationality, including Mexicans. In the Flores Magóns' case, the defense league planned to raise the $10,000 needed for bail. Rather incongruously, the group established its temporary headquarters in the American Bank Building in Los Angeles.[48]

Meanwhile, the legal battle had already begun. Defense attorney Ryckman filed a demurrer, claiming none of the material on which the charges were based tended to incite assassination or murder.[49] Arguing before a large audience of supporters, the defense noted the government ignored the important difference between rhetoric and performance. Ryckman drew a comparison between the Flores Magóns and abolitionist William Lloyd Garrison, whose remarks in the antislavery journal, the *Liberator,* made PLM rhetoric appear mild. Assistant United States Attorney Gallagher, in response, charged that the articles listed in the grand jury's indictment implied a conspiracy between President Wilson and Carranza at the expense of the people, and that such incendiary remarks led to the recent raid on Columbus, New Mexico. Furthermore, the prosecution believed such treasonous statements constituted a dagger aimed at the "hearts of both the American and Mexican governments."[50] Judge Benjamin F. Bledsoe voiced some doubts on the first two counts; however, since Mexico was currently torn by revolution, he concluded that such rhetoric might well be considered obscene. Apparently, the judge had no reservations on the third count. The court overruled the demurrer on all counts as well as a subsequent motion to quash the indictment.[51]

The defense continued to press for bail reductions, especially in view of Ricardo's deteriorating health; Ricardo Flores Magón appeared to be suffering from nervousness and general strain characterized by a defense doctor as neurasthenia. A government physician examined Flores Magón and confirmed his nervousness, but minimized the health danger.[52] A requested reduction of bail of $2,500 met with vigorous opposition from Assistant United States District Attorney Clyde R. Moody, who indicated the government would oppose reduction even if the defendant appeared to be dying. Again, the prosecution cited Pancho Villa's New Mexico raid, alleging that numerous copies of Regeneración had been sent to Columbus before the incident and the release of the defendants might lead to the killing of "some other good Americans" because of the inflammatory nature of their newspaper.[53] In fact, the mailing lists of Regeneración, introduced as evidence during the trial, did not include any subscribers in Columbus, New Mexico.[54] Moreover, such an argument ignored the fact that the Flores Magóns condemned Pancho Villa as just another parasite on the main body of the social revolution—the people. Presiding Judge Oscar A. Trippet denied bail reduction, although he agreed that Flores Magón's health required attention at the Los Angeles county hospital, where proper care and diet could be assured. In another preliminary move, the defense unsuccessfully requested that Ricardo's case be separated from his brother's and from the fugitive Owen's on the grounds that as a mere writer Flores Magón had nothing to do with the actual mailing of the newspaper.[55]

The inability of the Los Angeles radical community to raise bail forced the men to remain jailed during the entire trial. Obviously, interest in the Flores Magón case was not great among those that normally rallied around such issues. Alexander Berkman, aware of the lack of interest, chided militants for their failure to respond, especially since the primary issue involved freedom of the press—an issue of "direct concern" to labor. Union politicians, presumably the AFL might be too busy ingratiating themselves with capital to pay much attention to the Flores Magóns, but surely radicals realized that it was in their interest to save the brothers from the "master's bloodhounds." In an effort to shame them into action, Berkman observed that he personally knew a number of individuals in Los Angeles who could, if they desired, supply bail bond.[56]

The importance of the supression of *Regeneración* and other radical papers had been brought home to Berkman with the exclusion of issues nine and ten of the *Blast* from the mails because of an article on birth control considered "too strong" by the Post Office. Clearly, Berkman himself was vulnerable to a charge of violation of section 211 of the penal code. Free speech, he noted resignedly, exists for those who espouse approved ideas, but not for those whose ideas threaten the established order.[57]

On the eve of the trial, the *Blast* carried a photograph of the Flores Magóns on the front page, with Ricardo, looking every inch the intellectual, seated at his desk, pencil in hand. An editorial by Edgecomb Pinchon of the defense league praised the Flores Magóns' contribution to freedom, not only in Mexico, but throughout the world—linking their trial with the issue of freedom of the press. Pinchon, like Berkman, hoped to appeal to the broad spectrum of the Left; indeed, the league insisted that while many of its supporters disagreed with the PLM, they believed in the survival of the radical press. The league's function was to defend, not to spread propaganda—"today an anarchist, tomorrow a socialist, and the day after an industrialist."[58]

Meanwhile, the defense hoped to be able to separate the actions of the two brothers, perhaps obtaining at least one acquittal. By contending that Ricardo, as a mere literary contributor, could not be held responsible for the newspaper's publication or distribution, the defense attempted to place him under the protection of the first amendment safeguarding freedom of speech. In Enrique's case, the defense hoped to show that the language used in *Regeneración* was innocuous, and that willful depositing of obscene matter in the United States mails had not occurred.

Prosecution lawyers then had to prove Ricardo's connection to the editorial board and distribution of the newspaper as well as the allegation that it constituted a willful deposit of obscene nonmailable material. In an effort to do just that, the government called Ricardo's stepdaughter, Lucille, to the stand. As the *Times* reported, she proved to be a "tartar" of a witness, refusing to answer the question of exactly who bore the managerial responsibilities for *Regeneración*, and stamping her feet in defiance. Threatened with contempt of court, she admitted having observed Ricardo writing in the office of the newspaper.[59] United States Marshal C. T. Walton testified that Enrique stated previously both brothers owned the paper with the object of spreading anarchist propaganda. The government hoped that such testimony would destroy the elder Flores Magón's claim to being a mere writer. To establish the fact that *Regeneración* had been deposited and distributed through the mails, the prosecution introduced the newspaper's mailing list and copies of mailing slips. Translations of allegedly obscene articles were then presented to the court.[60]

The relentless presentation of the government's case before the court must have been depressing for the defendants. Friendly courtroom spectators, who suffered the indignity of being subjected to a weapons search before entering, offered the only source of support. Among those attending was Alexander Berkman, who lavishly praised the Flores Magóns im-

mediately after their arrest in his San Francisco publication as
rare individuals of a type seldom produced outside Russia
and Mexico.[61]

Both brothers took the stand in their own defense. Enrique
made a strong statement concerning his political beliefs, appealing to the jury to recognize that the poor merely desired
a share of that held by the more fortunate, and emphasizing
that he alone owned, edited, and managed the newspaper.
He reviewed the long personal struggle of both Flores Magóns for the social betterment of the Mexican people, and
boldly declared they had become anarchists with goals that
went beyond the "Mexican race" to encompass the "human
race," who should have the means to enjoy life as did the
Guggenheims or Rockefellers. Ricardo's statement, because
of ill health, lacked the spirit of his brother's response. He
characterized himself as just a literary contributor suffering
from diabetes and mental exhaustion.[62]

Assistant United States Attorney Mansel G. Gallaher,
mindful of the danger of becoming mired in legal distinctions
or technicalities, constantly interjected with emotional assess-
ments of anarchism. In response to Enrique's testimony, Gallaher noted that wealthy men owned thousands of acres in
Baja California, but that did not give anyone the right to hold
a revolver at their heads, compelling them to deed the land
to peons; after all, one must pay for something of value. The
selection of Baja California as an example was motivated by
the fact that California interests, including General Harrison
Gray Otis of the *Los Angeles Times* and his son-in-law, Harry
Chandler, as well as others, owned land on the Mexican side
of the border and entertained grandiose plans for development without regard to international borders. Gallaher denounced the brothers as proponents of murder making a
parasitic living off the misguided poor by deluding them into
the belief that they would receive free land in exchange for
their pitifully small financial contributions. The prosecution
linked past actions to the future characterizing the Flores Magóns as community menaces bound to cause serious social
problems unless convicted.[63]

Gallaher's highly charged rhetoric appeared believable to a public conditioned to equate anarchism with violence. In 1914 and 1915 a number of highly publicized bombings and bomb plots gripped the nation's attention. In New York an accidental explosion killed four anarchist friends of Alexander Berkman. Many believed their homemade bomb had been intended for John D. Rockefeller. A bomb blast set off to commemorate the Haymarket executions damaged the Bronx courthouse and two Italian anarchists, aided by a police *agent provocateur*, plotted to blow up St. Patrick's Cathedral. In the spring of 1916, as the Flores Magón case proceeded through the judicial process, yet another major anarchist scare swept the public imagination. Three hundred community leaders who had gathered at Chicago's University Club to honor Archbishop George W. Mundelein became violently ill after eating arsenic-laced chicken soup. Jean Crones, an immigrant and kitchen helper was held responsible. A raid on his living quarters revealed more vials of poison, explosives, and anarchist literature. Allegedly he was a friend of Gaetano Bresci, the Paterson, New Jersey, Italian immigrant responsible for the assassination of the Italian king in 1900. Newspapers linked all such stories into a nationwide pattern and conspiracy aimed at well-known political and economic figures. Gallaher's charge that the brothers were proponents of murder thus fell on responsive ears.[64]

Unsuccessfully, the defense argued that the jury should consider both the question of whether the language could be judged obscene and, as a separate consideration, whether or not the defendants had knowingly or willfully deposited non-mailable materials. The defense clearly stressed the jury's responsibility to be convinced beyond a reasonable doubt, or acquit the defendants. Judge Trippet, however, declined to instruct the jury in the manner requested by the defense.[65] The government's successful efforts to avoid the introduction of the principle of free speech were reflected in the panel's deliberations. In the morning, the jurors listened to Ryckman's final argument, including his definition of bourgeoisie, apparently in an attempt to distinguish those considered exploiters by the Flores Magóns. The jury, after listening to the court's instructions, retired from the courtroom at 10:28, ate lunch at 11:55, returned, and by four o'clock, reentered the courtroom with the verdict.[66] Such rapid deliberation indicated that the principle of free speech was not considered seriously, nor were they overawed by the fact that the case was the first brought to trial that dealt with the government's definition of obscenity as an act tending to incite murder, arson, and assassination.

The Flores Magóns and their supporters expected the worst. To Alexander Berkman, the trial demonstrated the futility of revolutionists attempting to defend themselves through legal technicalities—one could make a proud stand, demonstrate solidarity, and no more. To publicly demonstrate their refusal to bow before the power of the state, Ricardo accepted a bouquet of roses from his stepdaughter after a presentation speech by Berkman.[67] As the jury returned to the courtroom, supporters crushed back inside, mingling with special officers intent on avoiding any violent display. The verdict found the defendants not guilty on the first count, but guilty on the second and third counts. Lucille held her father's hand as the clerk read the verdict, clutching his hand convulsively, while Ricardo and Enrique appeared distraught and pale.[68] Ryckman immediately served notice that he intended to file a motion to arrest judgment before sentencing by Judge Trippet on June 12.

To support the arrest of judgment, the defense, besides alleging that the Flores Magóns' action did not constitute an offense against the United States, maintained that Congress, in amending the penal code of 1910 to define indecent matter, did not intend to deny the use of the mails to Mexicans, or others pressing for social change. Moreover, the defense questioned Congress' right to enact laws that appeared to infringe on the first amendment rights of the constitution.[69] Judge Trippet, responding to Ryckman, laid aside the matter of free speech and press, choosing to see the central question as the right of the government to protect itself. The judge conceded the point that Thomas Jefferson and Thomas Paine are considered patriots only because the revolt against England succeeded. In the case of the Flores Magóns, Judge Trippet observed that they had been in the country sixteen years, supposedly hiding behind the United States flag, when they should have been in Mexico fighting for their beliefs.

In response, Enrique, first explaining that his brother's illness prevented him from rebutting the judge's comments, attempted to place the PLM's activities, and the trial itself, in a broader perspective. Enrique noted that court records did not reflect the true nature of the PLM's struggle for Mexican proletarians in particular, and those of the world in general. Although their revolutionary ideals called for the destruction of the state's institutional structure, such beliefs were based on principles of justice and freedom. For the court to pass sentence would be to deny the Mexican people the right to revolt against unbearable conditions. Mexico's assets had been sold "for a mere song" to the "Otises, Hearsts, Rockefellers, Morgans, Guggenheims, and Pearsons," leaving individual Mexicans chattel slaves in their own land.[70] While the PLM's methods might not be universally pleasing, they at least had the approval of Thomas Jefferson, Enrique quoted, "we cannot expect to pass from despotism to liberty on a feather bed." Enrique declared Thomas Jefferson to be the anarchist of his day. By invoking Jefferson, Enrique demonstrated how much he had become an American anarchist. Thomas Jefferson's ambivalence about government and political power provided anarchists with innumerable quotes. The mantle of the American revolution could be used to refute the common charge that anarchism lacked native roots and existed only as an ideological delusion of a few maladjusted immigrants.

In reply to the judge's condemnation of their continued residence in the United States when the fight awaited them in Mexico, Enrique noted that the world was their country, and while they themselves were Mexicans, "our minds are not so narrow, our vision not so pitifully small" to regard others as aliens or enemies because of their place of birth. Since the Mexican revolution went beyond a single political movement to the country's social and economic roots, people had to be educated in order to identify the actual causes of their misery and determine the way to freedom. *Regeneración*, in spite of being published in Los Angeles, was not removed from the struggle, but central to the revolution. Enrique quoted Emerson on the ability of the intellectual to make "tyrants tremble." Whatever the court would decide, history, watching "from her throne" as the "social drama" unfolded, would in the end judge. Noting that poor health had claimed them both, Enrique speculated that another penitentiary term might be a death sentence. Then, dramatically, he concluded, "Let the court speak! History watches!"[71]

Enrique's eloquent address failed to deter the court, although Judge Trippet willingly conceded that the defense had been brilliant and the trial itself flawless. The judge overruled the motion for arrest of judgment as well as the motion for a new trial, which had been based on the court's refusal to separate Ricardo's from his brother's case. Judge Trippet set sentencing for June 22, 1916.[72] If Enrique's eloquence failed to move the court, the pleas for leniency on health grounds had an impact. Ricardo's generally poor physical condition, as well as his diabetes, concerned Judge Trippet. Much to Gallaher's disgust, the judge privately indicated that he would consider suspending sentencing if Flores Magón permanently left the country. Trippet believed that a possible ten-year sentence would discourage any return to American jurisdiction. Firmly opposing such an idea, the government attorney insisted that Flores Magón would receive better medical treatment in federal custody. Moreover, Gallaher claimed that the Flores Magóns would retreat to the Mexican side of the border, just out of reach of American judicial officers, and use the United States mails to continue their propaganda campaign against the American government. Obviously, Gallaher considered the Flores Magóns a purely American political problem that necessarily had to be dealt with by imprisonment. Trippet remained unconvinced, prompting Gallaher to ask Washington to pressure the judge.[73]

Federal authorities publicly indicated their desires to obtain a five-year term on each count. However, Judge Trippet, in what the *Times* called "extreme leniency," sentenced Enrique to a $1,000 fine and three years on each count to run concurrently, while Ricardo received an identical monetary fine and, because of his poor health, a year and a day on each count to run concurrently. The court set bail at $3,000 for Ricardo and $5,000 for his brother, pending appeal to the United States Circuit Court of Appeals.[74]

Raising bail seemed to be an impossible task until Emma Goldman, on one of her numerous lecture tours, arrived in Los Angeles and led the effort. She declared that her visit would be an utter failure unless the Flores Magóns were released. With characteristic energy, Goldman, aided by Alexander Berkman, quickly obtained surety bonds for the imprisoned men.[75] The Flores Magóns publicly thanked them in the July 20, 1916, issue of *Regeneración*.[76] Matilda Reuben Forrester of La Canada and Chauncy D. Clark of Los Angeles posted Ricardo's bail only two days after sentencing.[77] Enrique waited until July 1, when C.R.W. Richard Bruns and Mary R. Clark pledged acceptable bonds. A delegation of Los Angeles socialists accompanied Bruns and Clark as they arranged for Enrique's release, cheering as he walked out, temporarily a free man.[78]

That very evening, as guests of honor, Ricardo and Enrique Flores Magón attended a dance to raise defense funds for David Kaplin, who had been charged with complicity in the *Times* bombing. Enrique addressed the crowd and a chorus of girls sang a number of Mexican songs. With the Flores Magóns present, the benefit took on a triumphant air that must have been exceedingly heartening for the two men after the frustrations and discouragement of the trial.[79] Subsequently, Enrique, "our beloved Mexican comrade," in an attempt to repay Berkman for his unwavering support, spoke at a San Francisco rally in commemoration of the Haymarket anarchists. Ricardo, still very ill, did not attend. The *Blast* sympathetically suggested that someone should see to it that the "Kropotkin of Mexico" receive the medical treatment he so desperately needed.[80]

Meanwhile, the International Workers Defense League of Los Angeles, previously organized with author Edgecomb Pinchon as general secretary, "in the service of those captured by the enemy," began the task of raising appeal funds. The defense league circular included supportive statements from Emma Goldman, Alexander Berkman, and Edgecomb Pinchon, listed as coauthor with Berkman of a suppressed book titled *The Mexican People: Their Struggle for Freedom.* Katherine L. Schmidt, sister of one of the men convicted of the *Los Angeles Times* bombing, served as treasurer.[81] Dr. T. Percival Gerson, a prominent Los Angeles physician and member of the liberal Severance Club, invited both the Flores Magóns and Ryckman to address the club at one of their bimonthly meetings. Dr. Gerson had followed the case closely, and in fact had examined the ill Ricardo in the county jail. The invitation to the Severance Club offered the men an opportunity to plead their case before some of the most important liberals in Southern California.[82]

As the appeals process moved slowly through the judicial system, a new factor began to complicate the political survival of the Flores Magóns. With the United States' entrance into the world war imminent, the government became increasingly concerned with internal security, especially after the discovery and publication of the Zimmermann telegram, which promised to return Mexico's northern territories in exchange for Mexico's cooperation with Germany against the United States.[83] The *Los Angeles Times* reported that prudent protective measures in times of war had drawn the authorities' attention to the "new nest of notorious anarchists" situated just outside the city limits at the Pacific Electric power town of Ivanhoe. Allegedly all manner of "riffraff," including Wobblies and anarchists, had gathered at that location. The *Times* speculated that should German agents manage to combine with Villistas to harass the United States, presumably by raiding the border, the anarchists would be sure to assist them.[84]

Speeches by Ricardo's wife, María, and stepdaughter, Lucille, at the downtown plaza on two consecutive Sunday afternoons to a largely Spanish-speaking crowd were viewed as new attempts to incite violence, and prompted an even closer watch on the anarchist group. These April 1917 appearances of Ricardo Flores Magón's female family members, which occurred shortly after the United States formally entered the war, heightened the internal security aspects of the incidents. Police concern over such public activities eventually led to the arrest of Raúl Palma, Lucille's companion, and several others. Both women managed to disappear into the crowd as soon as the arrests began. The Federal Immigration Service announced it expected to secure the deportation of those arrested.[85] Official intimidation was expected to discourage such political gatherings in the future.

On February 4, 1918, the U.S. Circuit Court of Appeals upheld the lower court's conviction of the Flores Magóns. The central issue, that the alleged uncertainty of the definition of "indecent" voided the statute because it permitted excessively arbitrary power to decide which words tended to incite murder or assassination, was not accepted by the appeals court. While acknowledging the amendment created a new dimension, the court held that the statute itself had been established previously—it was no more difficult to decide whether language tended to incite murder or assassination than whether or not it might corrupt morals. The definition contained in the criminal code appeared to the court to be sufficiently clear to permit prosecution. Whether or not the defendants knew the deposited material to be indecent was held irrelevant, since lack of intent could not be used as a defense. The court ruled that Judge Trippet, in refusing to instruct the jury to acquit if they believed the defendants had been unaware of the indecent character of their published remarks, acted correctly. To support its view, the circuit court quoted from a United States Supreme Court opinion in a moral obscenity case:

> Congress did not intend that the question as to the character of the paper should depend upon the opinion or belief of the person . . . since the evils . . . would continue and increase in volume, if the belief of the accused as to what was obscene,

lewd, and lascivious was recognized as the test for determining whether the statute has been violated.

The appeal judges made no attempt to separate moral obscenity from the political question, which touched directly on the constitutional guarantees of freedom of speech and press.[86] As a result, defense attorney Ryckman filed his intention to appeal to the Supreme Court because of the alleged constitutional issues involved.[87]

Little more than two months later, on April 19, 1918, a new indictment was issued against Ricardo Flores Magón and Librado Rivera. Enrique avoided indictment because a disagreement with his brother over tactics had resulted in his resignation from *Regeneración*'s editorial board; however, under the 1916 conviction, his commitment to McNeil Island was issued on May 18, 1918, although he served the sentence at Leavenworth[88] together with his brother.

5

Los Angeles, 1918

The PLM had become increasingly irrelevant to the political situation in Mexico. Venustiano Carranza, self-appointed first chief of the Constitionalists, succeeded in using, then crushing, the anarchistic *Casa del Obrero Mundial* before mobilizing labor to support his presidential campaign. On May Day of 1917 he recognized the legality of unions and the eight-hour day. A series of presidential decrees increasing wages and the turning of Mexico City's tram system over to the workers appeared to be concrete proof of Carranza's sincere support for the working class. Consequently, many shifted their active allegiance to Carranza. Individual friends and former supporters of Ricardo Flores Magón such as Antonio I. Villarreal, who had been arrested along with the Flores Magón brothers in the police raid on the PLM Los Angeles headquarters, and Juan Sarabia, at one time a committed follower, now backed Carranza.[1] Even Emiliano Zapata who remained ideologically close to Ricardo Flores Magón had established his own revolutionary persona and program. Zapata, as did the PLM's leadership, bitterly rejected Carranza's limited reforms, but he did so as an independent leader. Moreover, Emiliano Zapata's day-to-day involvement in the armed struggle stood in sharp contrast to Ricardo Flores Magón's absence.

To many former supporters of the PLM it appeared fruitless to hold out for ideological purity when the Mexican government seemed prepared to implement at least partly many long-standing goals. Ricardo Flores Magón thus became a living revolutionary icon now elevated above the real struggle where deals were made and principles adjusted to meet sometimes less than honorable objectives. Flores Magón in exile appeared more of a detached spiritual force—an ideological deity. His continued martyrdom seemed both predictable and fitting to many of his former comrades in Mexico. Only in the United States was he viewed as an active, dangerous political figure and then mostly in the minds of judicial authorities. Ricardo Flores Magón's arrest and subsequent trial in 1918 must be viewed as part of the pattern of repression that accompanied World War I. As an anarchist, associated with socialists and the IWW, Flores Magón could not escape persecution. He would not be considered a "Mexican radical," but part of the general radicalism that threatened national security and jeopardized the war effort.

In the early months of 1917, the War Department instructed local army officials to repress seditious acts sternly and protect vital industries. Although President Wilson approved these measures, he asked Newton D. Baker, the Secretary of War, to ensure that military commanders distinguish between ordinary offenses and crimes committed with seditious intent. In order to promptly snuff out potential trouble before it could injure the war effort, military officials were to be responsive directly to local interests. Army units could be called upon to assist county sheriffs and district attorneys. Despite grave doubts expressed by the Secretary of Labor, William B. Wilson, a former congressman and UMW official, and the Justice Department, troops raided IWW offices, detained individuals without charges for weeks, and even patrolled towns. Soldiers used violence to break up meetings of suspected radicals, and military authorities searched freight trains, questioning individuals about their political opinions. In the summer of 1917, federal troops occupied the copper camps of Arizona and Montana and the suppression of strike activity became an important part of the army's overall domestic security campaign.[2] Military intelligence expanded, from two officers in early 1917 to more than 300 supported by 1,000 civilian employees by the end of the war.[3]

While authorities often cited the presence of IWW agitators as a pretext for such harsh measures, they rarely distinguished between groups perceived as socially and politically undesirable. Moreover, a conspiracy theory linking all elements of the Left emerged after the success of the Bolshevik Revolution in November 1917. Newspapers and magazines indiscriminately linked American radicals to Soviet revolutionaries, ignoring important philosophical differences between them. By the end of 1917, the *New York Times*, reflecting public hysteria, published a report on the alleged connection between domestic radicals and Soviet revolutionaries. The headline ran "See Worldwide Anarchist Plot," and the article's subtitle asserted that "Washington Officials Connect IWW, Bolsheviks, and the Revolutionaries in Many Lands."[4]

Under the circumstances, the PLM could not fail to draw the attention of the Justice Department. The intolerant and repressive atmosphere that resulted from the country's entry into the war had been predicted and even approved by President Wilson. According to the editor of the *New York World*, the President commented that the American people would become intolerant of leftist groups; indeed, in order to fight and win, one must be ruthless and brutal. Wilson predicted that such sentiments would penetrate "every fiber of our national life," from Congress to the courts, from local police departments to the man on the street. In a similar fashion, the socialist convention held in St. Louis recognized that the times had grown dangerous and understood that war provided a possible pretext and socially acceptable reason to attack the country's democratic institutions.[5]

Keenly aware of how difficult it would be to marshal public opinion in favor of a distant war, President Wilson viewed any opposition with alarm. Emotionally and intellectually, the country could have moved in either direction—pro- or anti-European involvement. Left to chance, the outcome remained uncertain. Even Wilson's own progressive supporters could not be expected to align themselves automatically with his war policy. All the authority and influence of the presidential office would have to be applied to rally support. A master at molding public opinion, Wilson never doubted that suitably educated and emotionally charged, the nation could be brought into line. As early as 1915, in his preparedness proposal to Congress, Wilson indicated the nature of his pro-war campaign when he condemned alleged foreign-born advocates of disloyalty and anarchy.[6]

After the United States entered the war, the President grew even more concerned with national security. His fear that a truculent working class might undermine industrial production and hinder military expansion approached paranoia. With the assistance of George Creel's Committee on Public Information—staffed by such notable muckrakers as Ida Tarbell, Ernest Poole, Will Irwin, and Ray Stannard—President Wilson hoped to create a climate of public opinion that would stimulate the unqualified support he believed necessary for pro-war politics. Although he and Creel publicly denounced vigilantism, they encouraged the emotional environment that made it possible. Moreover, Wilson made only halfhearted attempts to control the excesses of his own Postmaster General, Albert Sidney Burleson, a man who, according to Norman Thomas, "didn't know socialism from rheumatism."[7] Although President Wilson did not derive pleasure from doing what he felt the war demanded, he appeared willing to accept both positive and negative contributions in building a pro-war consensus. He did little to discourage the serious constitutional violations committed by public organizations and judicial authorities at every level. Consequently, a wave of patriotic intimidation swept the nation, one that claimed many victims—including Ricardo Flores Magón.

On April 19, 1918, the federal district court in Los Angeles indicted Ricardo Flores Magón and Librado Rivera for conspiracy to violate the Espionage Act of 1917, the Trading with the Enemy Act, and the amended Federal Penal Code of 1910.[8] Under the Espionage Act, individuals who during times of war circulate false statements or reports with the intent to interfere with military operations, cause insubordination, disloyalty or mutiny, or obstruct recruitment or enlistment would be subject to a maximum $10,000 fine and twenty years' imprisonment. The Act also declared "every letter, writing, circular, postal card, picture, print, engraving, photo-

graph, newspaper, pamphlet, book, or other publication matter, or thing of any kind" in violation of the Espionage Act
to be nonmailable and subject to separate penalties of one to
five years and a $5000 fine.[9]
With similar intent, the Trading with the Enemy Act singled out publications; declaring it illegal to print, or cause to
be printed, published, or circulated, in a foreign language any
editorial or news item concerning policies, international relations, or conduct of the war by the United States or any nation engaged in the conflict without filing a legal translation,
which must be approved prior to circulation. The law provided a maximum penalty of one year, a $500 fine, and, in
addition, violation of the Trading with the Enemy Act also
placed the individual in violation of the Espionage Act of 1917
and thus subject to the penalties it provided.[10] The third law
allegedly violated, the amended Federal Penal Code, had
been successfully utilized against Flores Magón in 1916.

Federal officials considered the monitoring of mass communications the most effective way to control suspected subversive elements. Radical newspapers and periodicals seldom
had sufficient local support to survive; consequently, they
had to appeal to a national audience, inevitably involving use
of the United States mails. Although the penal code by itself
proved to be a formidable weapon, wartime hysteria demanded even more control. With great satisfaction, the Postmaster General reported that the Espionage Act, together
with the Trading with the Enemy Act, gave his department
a way of dealing with seditious material and other "more or
less disloyal" publications that attempted to utilize the mails.
Later, the United States Postal Service claimed to be exercis-
ing great care in issuing licenses to foreign-language newspapers under the authority of the Trading with the Enemy
Act to guard against the circulation of "seditious utterances."
At the same time, it adopted a policy of "great liberality" toward criticism and free expression not deemed a threat to the
national welfare. Monitoring of foreign-language material
depended, to a large extent, on several hundred profes-
sors of modern languages from colleges and universities

throughout the country who "patriotically volunteered" their services.[11]

In the case of Flores Magón, the specific act on which the indictment based its complaints concerned a manifesto published in *Regeneración* on March 16, 1918. Addressed to the "Organizing Junta of the Mexican Liberal Party (PLM), Anarchists of the World and Workers in General," the manifesto allegedly contained false statements. By supposedly interfering with military operations, inciting disloyalty and mutiny, and obstructing enlistment and recruiting, it violated the provisions of the Espionage Act. Furthermore, no English translation had been filed with the Post Office, and the manifesto allegedly contained indecent matter and language. The first count charged that Flores Magón and Rivera had conspired to violate these laws but left actual violations to be listed in subsequent counts of the indictment.

To sustain the charge of criminal commission, the second count selected and interpreted rhetorical statements contained in the manifesto in a literal fashion: "The death of the old society is close at hand, it will not delay much longer and only those will deny the fact whom its continuation interests" was declared to mean that the United States government "was then and there moribund." Selecting a paragraph observing that "the working man goes on strike not taking in account that by his action, he injures the country's interest, conscious now that the country is not his property, but is the property of the rich," the second count charged it falsely implied that the working man had no part or ownership interest in the country. More revolutionary, at least in language, was the paragraph that stated:

> the flames of discontent revived by the blow of tyranny each time [becoming] more enraged and cruel in every country and here, and there, everywhere and in all parts; the fists contract, the mind exalts, the hearts beat violently, and where they do not murmur, they shout, all sighing for the moment in which the calloused hands, during a hundred centuries of labor . . . must drop the fecund tools, and grab the rifle which nervously awaits the caress of the heroes.

To the grand jury, this excerpt suggested that its author found the United States so tyrannical that its citizens contemplated a revolutionary overthrow of the government. The jury declared all selected statements, suitably interpreted, to be falsely and willfully made with the intent to interfere with the operation and success of military forces, and to promote the enemy's cause.[12]

The third count—also based on the published manifesto—charged an attempt to incite insubordination, disloyalty, mutiny, and refusal of service by military personnel. Presumably, those who read it would be influenced to the point of withdrawing their support from the American war effort. The alleged mailing of nonmailable material resulted in a fourth count, based on a copy of *Regeneración* addressed to an individual in Guadalupe County, Texas, and a sixth count, based on a copy mailed to a person in Tampa, Florida. Failure to file a translation constituted the substance of the fifth count.[13]

Defense attorney Ryckman, joined by Chaim Shapiro and Sakharam Pandit, responded with a demurrer to all counts on the grounds that the facts did not support the charges and moreover, that the indictment appeared to be repetitious in as much as the manifesto constituted the substance of each separate charge. Ryckman objected to the characterization of the manifesto as a series of false statements when, in fact, it was merely opinion. The defense declared the manifesto to be "empty rhetoric, words,—words,—words,—words,—signifying nothing."[14] The defense's objection was sustained only on the second count—a slight victory, given the enormity of the government's case. The men entered not guilty pleas to all remaining charges.

Jury selection resulted in ten challenges and, ultimately, in the impanelment of twelve jurors chaired by A. A. Allen, proprietor of a Spring Street, Los Angeles, insurance agency.[15] Unfortunately, presiding Judge Benjamin F. Bledsoe had already earned a reputation for his broad interpretations of what constituted dangerously disloyal acts. In a celebrated 1917 case with the interesting title, "The United States vs. Motion Picture Film 'The Spirit of '76,'" Judge Bledsoe had acted against views that he considered detrimental to the war effort. The case involved a film produced by Robert Goldstein, an associate of D. W. Griffith, director of the well-known film, "The Birth of a Nation." The Goldstein film included such scenes as Patrick Henry's speech against taxation without representation and the signing of the Declaration of Independence. Completed shortly before the United States entered the war and shown to a Los Angeles audience, the film was strongly criticized and the government ultimately indicted Goldstein for presenting a view of British-American relations calculated to arouse antagonism, hatred, and enmity between active allies. The government considered the depiction of the Wyoming Valley Massacre particularly objectionable because it pictured British soldiers bayoneting women and children as well as carrying off girls. Seizure of the film and Goldstein's indictment ruined his production company. Goldstein recieved a ten-year sentence, which was later commuted to three years.[16] Judge Bledsoe reasoned that it was not necessary to prove the film's effect—supposedly that of weakening ties between allies and thus their chances of success—but merely to calculate it reasonably.[17]

Ryckman, aware of the antisubversive hysteria encouraged by the federal government, as well as Judge Bledsoe's reputation, fully realized the political nature of the Flores Magón case. Consequently, he attempted to argue on philosophical grounds, leaving the government to produce witnesses and go through the motions of documenting its case. The government called Emilio Kosterlitzky, then an interpreter and translator for the Justice Department, to the stand to testify that he had purchased a copy of *Regeneración* containing the manifesto at a newstand for five cents. Kosterlitzky had been a former naval cadet in the Imperial Russian Navy before jumping ship and beginning the life of a soldier of fortune. He had served Porfirio Díaz with distinction as a colonel in the *Rurales* stationed along the Sonora-Arizona border; he played an important role in border pacification and apprehension of PLM activists, as well as suppression of the Cananea strike in 1906. As chief of military intelligence for Sonora,

Sinaloa, and Baja California, Kosterlitzky was well acquainted with Ricardo Flores Magón. In fact, he stated that he had known the defendant for twenty years. After the collapse of the Porfiriato, Kosterlitzky served both Francisco Madero and Victoriano Huerta before taking refuge in the United States where, with the assistance of a friend in the Arizona Rangers, he obtained his Justice Department position. To the defendants, Colonel Kosterlitzky's appearance on the witness stand must have seemed like the shadow of the Porfiriato seeking long-delayed revenge.[18]

Julius Jansen, mail superintendent of the Los Angeles post office, testified that a legally required translation of the manifesto had not been filed; that copies of the newspaper actually had been deposited in the mails, where they had been impounded; and that two copies had been sent to the Postal Department in Washington, D.C. Postal inspector Walter M. Cookson further testified that all items bore the Los Angeles postmark. One copy offered as evidence, was addressed to an individual aboard the government revenue cutter, *McCullough*. Over defense objections, the prosecution read aloud from another copy, the July 28, 1917, edition of *Regeneración*, which contained an address by Ricardo Flores Magón delivered at the Italian Hall in Los Angeles for the International Workers Defense League. In the speech, Flores Magón called Mexican President Carranza a "lackey" of President Wilson and a "bandit of Wall Street," defending anarchist doctrines as dangerous only to the pocketbooks of "vampires" who "feed upon the worker." The speech questioned the value as well as the objectives of the war, and in it, Ricardo denounced wartime restrictions, declaring that "for tyranny, silence is a virtue" forcing the citizen to "see, hear, and hush."[19] By introducing the document as relevant evidence, the prosecution clearly intended to bolster the charge of violation of the Espionage Act, which, up to that point, had rested solely on the manifesto cited in the indictment.

To establish links between the defendants and other radicals, the government introduced Emma Goldman's open letter, "On the Way to Golgotha," as evidence; it had been reprinted in *Regeneración* (March 16, 1918). Again, the defense objected: the letter was inadmissible, irrelevant, immaterial, and only the opinion of a third party not binding on the defendants.[20] In order to lend some credence to the charge of interfering with military recruitment, the government had a local recruiting officer testify. Lieutenant Colonel William E. Purviance, Los Angeles army recruiting officer, stated that he was familiar with recruiting efforts around the time the manifesto appeared, and that a number of individuals of Mexican extraction enlisted in Los Angeles. On cross-examination, Colonel Purviance admitted that he had no idea whether any of the soldiers at Fort MacArthur or naval personnel at the San Pedro submarine base spoke or understood Spanish and could thus read *Regeneración*, since the military used English exclusively.[21] Nevertheless, the prosecution's interpretation of Purviance's testimony suggested a direct connection between the war effort and the allegedly seditious manifesto. Defense attorney Ryckman's cross-examination skillfully highlighted the prosecution's weak points, yet, because of the emotional climate, attempts to rule out irrelevant testimony proved unsuccessful. Only in the case of Fred Woodward, a newspaper reporter who testified that he had found copies of *Regeneración* on the steps of City Hall, supposedly thrown there by Rivera, was the defense's objection sustained—the witness failed to make a positive identification of the newspapers in question.[22] Ryckman constantly found himself arguing on two different levels. Philosophically, the defense argued that the alleged offense did not constitute a violation of the law; more pragmatically, the evidence presented by the prosecution could not be traced positively to the defendants. It soon became evident that the defense could not make any significant dent in the federal case. Low courtroom attendance by PLM supporters reflected the hopelessness of the situation.

Outside the courtroom, an "International Committee for the Defense of Magón and Rivera" had been formed in Los Angeles. Nicholas Senn Zogg served as treasurer and Raúl Palma acted as secretary. Senn Zogg carefully composed an appeal for funds which emphasized that justice required money. Ironically, this statement subsequently formed part of the basis for the indictment against both Senn Zogg and Palma.[23] Word of Flores Magón's arrest and the urgent need for funds was circulated in the radical press. Responding to a report published in the *New York Call*, the "Liberty Defense League," a nonpartisan group organized to defend civil liberties, came forth with limited financial support. Prominent liberals and radicals—including Max Eastman, Elizabeth Gurley Flynn, Norman M. Thomas, Eugene V. Debs, and David Starr Jordan, Chancellor of Stanford University—served on the executive or general committee of the Liberty Defense Union.[24] In Los Angeles, the Severance Club extended an invitation to Nicholas Senn Zogg to discuss defense efforts with its members—an indication of the interest of the Los Angeles liberal and socialist community in the case. Guy Bogart of the book review section of the *Citizen*, the official publication of organized labor in Los Angeles, extended permission to the Flores Magón defense committee to list Eugene V. Debs, Theodore Debs, and radical poet Ruth LePrade as members of the defense committee.[25] Such support, while heartening, did nothing to influence the direction of the judicial proceedings.

The trial ended unexpectedly when Ryckman informed the court that he would not call any witnesses, nor require Ricardo Flores Magón and Librado Rivera to testify. Judge Benjamin F. Bledsoe allotted the government an hour to summarize its case. The defense had an hour-and-a-half to conclude its case, in view of the lack of defense witnesses. In their closing statement, government lawyers emphasized the political nature of the case by characterizing the manifesto as a "palpable form of anarchy." Government attorney Lawson challenged the contention that anarchists could be considered pacifists. He played on the popular image held by the public when he posed the rhetorical question, "Have you ever seen or heard of an anarchist who was a pacifist? Anarchism in every sense of its meaning signifies violence." Flores Magón's association with Emma Goldman and Alexander Berkman, two well-known anarchists then serving prison terms, allegedly "showed the defendants' sympathy for them and proved beyond a reasonable doubt their antagonism to the conduct of the war."[26]

Ryckman's philosophical defense apparently moved Judge Bledsoe. In his jury instruction, Bledsoe went beyond legal formalities, indulging in "some reflections." Articulating his desire to avoid capricious criticism, he nevertheless called the defense's argument "almost childlike and bland in its simplicity." The judge found attempts to emphasize the fine points of anarchism ridiculous, especially the denial of the need for a government. Bledsoe even went so far as to question the perfectibility of human beings. Perhaps reflecting upon his years on the bench, the judge declared, "we are not perfect." As Bledsoe saw it, Ryckman's invocation of Thoreau's belief that the best government governs the least should be amended to include a statement "compatible with the general good." Warming to his subject, the judge spoke glowingly of Anglo-Saxon theory and the American tradition of a government of liberty—a liberty that had to be "kept within bounds by this other thing that we call law."[27]

Judge Bledsoe further noted that free speech and press, "speaking largely," is a right, yet one limited by public safety considerations. The judge cautioned the jury to ignore the suggestion that a government merely legalized the domination of one class. He also warned them to set aside the academic merits of anarchism. Judge Bledsoe declared the defendants to be dreamers, and while such idealistic individuals played a role in society, the state could not allow their dreams to turn into nightmares which adversely affected the community. In the case of "these anarchists," when they gave up dreaming and violated the law, it became a matter of subverting the government. Furthermore, the judge reminded the jury of the war: "the greatest war not only in which we have ever been involved, but the greatest war in which the world has ever been engaged." The gravity of the times, he said, this "supreme moment in history," required that unusual means be used to protect the state. In his reflections, Judge Bledsoe clearly communicated his personal opinion that in order to protect the United States government and society, the defendants should be found guilty.[28]

Returning to legal formalities, the judge explained the sections of each law that had been allegedly violated. He noted that in the case of section 211 of the Penal Code the jury could find a perfect example of how "wonderfully" Congress worked by defining "indecent" to mean tending to incite arson, murder, and assasination. Judge Bledsoe observed that while the word had been given a meaning entirely foreign to that commonly accepted, it hardly was intended for the lexicographer.[29] The judge's amusement did not imply any disagreement with the justness of such an expanded definition. For its part, the defense approached the jury with instructions that were very formal and legalistic. Apparently convinced that any further abstract defense would be fruitless, Ryckman concentrated on the legal notion of reasonable doubt. He attempted to convince the jury that finding the defendants guilty beyond a reasonable doubt would prove extremely difficult, particularly on the grounds of circulating a manifesto that intended to violate the law.[30]

Nevertheless, almost anyone could have predicted the final verdict. After deliberating for only two hours, the jury found both defendants guilty on all counts. The verdict was read to an almost-empty courtroom; even Ryckman failed to appear. Ricardo Flores Magón's stepdaughter, Lucille Norman, and Rivera's family offered what support they could to the convicted men. Subsequently, the defense filed a motion to arrest judgment that was quickly overruled.[31]

Before closing the case entirely, Judge Bledsoe noted that the defendants' previous federal convictions indicated their persistent violation of the law: They deserved no pity. Viewing the defendants as dangerous radicals, he solemnly declared that "these men and their kind are not to be allowed to hold a copy of the Constitution in one hand and a knife to stab it to death in the other." Free speech did not extend "license" to destroy the Constitution.[32] Thus in defense of the state, Ricardo Flores Magón received a $5,000 fine and two years' imprisonment on the first count (conspiracy). On the third count (the second having been ruled out), which charged an attempt to incite insubordination and refusal of military service, the judge imposed $5,000 and twenty years' confinement. The fourth and sixth charges each resulted in a $5,000 fine and five years, and the fifth count in one day in the Los Angeles County jail. All sentences were to run concurrently following the expiration of a year and a day imposed as a result of the earlier case, and one $5,000 fine would also be considered to be sufficient monetary punishment. The court then set bond at $50,000 pending appeal. Librado Rivera received an identical sentence except on the third count where his term was set at fifteen years.[33]

Ryckman filed an appeal with the United States Circuit Court of Appeals in San Francisco on the grounds of a repetitious indictment that charged the defendants with an act that could not be considered an offense against the United States. The appeal also stated that the local trial had erroneously admitted evidence that was not directly related to the charges. Speaking for the court, Circuit Judge Ross agreed that all the offenses stemmed from one transaction. However, he argued that several counts listed in one indictment did not constitute repetition. He observed that while only one crime, conspiracy, appeared to be involved, the separate counts listed violation of three separate and specific provisions of federal statute and, therefore, could not be considered redundant.

After disposing of the technical questions, the court considered the less than clear-cut issue of the admissibility of evidence.[34] With regard to the prosecution's introduction of Ricardo Flores Magón's March 27, 1917, speech—the one published in *Regeneración* on July 28 of the same year—and Emma Goldman's letter of February 6, 1918, published in the March 6, 1918, issue of PLM's newspaper, the court agreed on the need for an interpretive judgment. Examining a part of the speech (out of context) which read:

> hurt all of those who live from the labor of others; our words hurt the parasites, the useless and noxious beings who suck the blood of the people; the clergymen, the bourgeois, and the

ruler; these are the ones who are injured by our words. So much the worse for them, so much the better for us! That the country is at war, and that is why we cannot talk. Bully reason this!

The court identified the defendants' central contention to be that free speech in time of war did not differ from that allowed at any other time. Citing precedent, as well as a Supreme Court ruling, the Court of Appeals declared this to be an incorrect assumption. Selecting another segment of the published speech that declared:

> We, the anarchists, cannot shut up; we shall not shut up. So long as injustice reigns, our voice shall be heard. . . . Go on, you haughty overlords, swallow your order, for we the anarchists, are not disposed to obey it; we cannot shut up, we will not shut up, and we shall speak. Cost what it may. . . . Above your caprice is our right, right which we do not owe to you, but to nature, which has endowed us with a mind to think, and in the defense of a right, understand it well, we are ready for anything, and to face it all, be it the dungeon or the gallows. Don't forget that right, no matter how much you may mutilate it, no matter how much you may crush it, no matter how much you may try to annihilate it, when it is persecuted the most, and when you are proudest of your triumph, it roars its vengeance in dynamite belches lead from the barricade.

The court ruled that Flores Magón's rhetoric showed hostile intent. Therefore, its introduction during the trial was correct. Ricardo's speech, coupled with Emma Goldman's letter, which ended with "good-bye dear friends, but not for long—if the spirit of the Bolsheviki prevails. Long live the Bolsheviki! May their flames spread over the world and redeem humanity from its bondage!" appeared to advocate violence and revolution—therefore, the judges found that it had a direct bearing on establishing the intent of the convicted men. The United States Circuit Court of Appeals fully affirmed the lower court's judgment when it handed down its decision on October 6, 1919.[35] With apparent satisfaction, the *Los Angeles Times* recalled that Ricardo Flores Magón had been the "head center" of local agitators seeking to "entrench Bolshevism" in the United States, but reported that his "disciples of unrest" had failed.[36]

The same month the circuit court rejected Flores Magón's appeal, preliminary deportation proceedings began against his brother, Enrique. Sentenced to what amounted to a life term, Ricardo had already been taken care of to the satisfaction of the Justice Department. Two of Flores Magón's stalwart supporters also fell victim to antiradical hysteria. The unprecedented deportation campaign of 1919–1920—orchestrated by J. Edgar Hoover—claimed Emma Goldman and Alexander Berkman among its victims. Highlighted by the expulsion of 249 alleged radicals, including Goldman and Berkman, aboard the "Buford" (dubbed the "Soviet Ark" by officials) in December 1919, the campaign became a national media event.[37] Enrique avoided deportation until March 1923, despite his release from Leavenworth in September 1920.[38] Assistant Secretary of Labor Louis F. Post, an outspoken critic of the Bureau of Investigation's heavy-handed tactics, refused to approve hasty and possibly illegal deportations. Several congressional committees investigated his alleged interference with deportation efforts. Post defended his handling of the Enrique Flores Magón case on the grounds that it could not be established that Enrique was a dangerous anarchist and, moreover, that his life might be endangered if he returned to Mexico.[39]

Ironically, Enrique's own account states that he received a hero's welcome when he crossed from El Paso, Texas, into Ciudad Juárez. Encouraged by the crowd, he made an impassioned speech that questioned the progress of the Mexican revolution and attacked the army. Uneasy police authorities debated how to silence him without antagonizing those who viewed him and his brother Ricardo as revolutionary martyrs. Well aware of the revolution's politics, Enrique believed that President Alvaro Obregón could not take that political risk. Years later, he related a story, supposedly passed on by someone close to Obregón: When Mexico City's chief of police discussed arresting Enrique, the President exploded,

"The entire nation has its eyes fixed on Flores Magón and a cretin like you wants to arrest him!"[40] Enrique continued agitating in Mexico until October 25, 1954, when he died. Political notables as well as the more humble observed his passing, the latter with sorrow.

6

Loose Ends:
Los Angeles, 1918

The government underscored its intention of destroying *Regeneración* and all those associated with it by indicting and arresting Flores Magón's wife, María. Epigmenio Zavala, also indicted with her, became a fugitive, subsequently fleeing to Mexico. María Flores Magón had been placed on the newspaper's editorial board as a result of Enrique Flores Magón's resignation, thereby attracting the attention of federal officials. It is doubtful that her role in the PLM changed with the appointment. The government, however, well aware of the importance of women in radical politics, hoped to eliminate the possibility that her husband's cause would continue to create difficulties under María's stewardship. Lucille Norman, María's daughter, had been scheduled to take over the English-language page as a result of Owen's flight, but she escaped indictment since she had been unable to assume that responsibility because of the emotional stress caused by the arrest of her companion, Raúl Palma, on a trumped-up murder charge.[1] María's arrest occurred just as Ricardo's trial neared its end. Still presiding over Flores Magón's case, Judge Bledsoe signed the bench warrant on July 12, 1918, and María was apprehended the following day.[2]

In addition to naming María Flores Magón and Epigmenio Zavala, the indictment charged various and sundry unknown individuals with conspiracy; the government intended to throw the net as wide as possible. The grand jury charged María with precisely the same violation for which Ricardo and Librado Rivera then stood trial.[3] In support of the alleged conspiracy, the grand jury singled out the manifesto of March

93

6, 1918, (addressed to the "Members of the Party [PLM], the Anarchists of all the Whole World, and Workingmen in general") published in the March 16, 1918, edition of *Regeneración*, which had been introduced in Ricardo Flores Magón's trial. The fact that only Flores Magón and Rivera had signed the manifesto appeared to be a minor technicality that could be easily overcome by demonstrating María's support of her husband's position.

To tie María Flores Magón directly in with the alleged conspiracy, the grand jury listed a number of letters which had been deposited in the mails, and then presumably ferreted out and removed by the Post Office's efficient censors. The first letter, addressed to Francisco Aonte Acasio and postmarked April 10, 1918, hardly supported the charge of a dangerous conspiracy. Essentially, the letter was María's denunciation of those who had failed to support her husband. In it, she wrote of the split between the Flores Magón brothers voicing the opinion that "Ricardo's ideals are far superior to Enrique's." In fact, she believed that there had never been an affinity between their ideas. She maintained that *Regeneración* was "sustained during many years by the brain of Ricardo and not through any influence of Enrique." María bitterly denounced Antonio Villarreal, Juan Sarabia, Romulo Carmona, Enrique's father-in-law, as well as Ricardo's elder brother, Jesús, for being obscure individuals of slight prestige, interested only in taking advantage of her husband. Although the letter included a few caustic references to the United States, such as that "classic republic of liberty, the model republic of the United States," the Justice Department actually should have been comforted by its contents because it indicated Ricardo's growing isolation as well as the virtual collapse of the PLM.[4]

The second letter, addressed to Leopoldo Valencia, reported the acquittal of Raúl Palma, and included a number of references to her editorial responsibility for the newspaper. More to the point of the indictment, it characterized the war as meaningless to the workers. The grand jury also linked the fugitive Zavala to the conspiracy by virtue of his having mailed a copy of a circular in his capacity as secretary for the Committee for the Defense of the Editor of *Regeneración*, which appealed for funds and enclosed a copy of the manifesto.[5]

A new indictment, filed August 19, 1918, named María Flores Magón, Epigmenio Zavala, Nicholas Senn Zogg, and Raúl Palma (along with various parties unknown) for violation of three counts of the Espionage Act.[6] Bail was set at $10,000 each. Once again, the authorities listed the manifesto of March 6, 1918, in support of the conspiracy charge. Circulars deposited in the mails, along with copies of *Regeneración* containing the manifesto, were brought forward. A circular dated May 13, 1918, and postmarked June 25 of the same year was entered in support of the charge. Signed by Senn Zogg as Treasurer and Raúl Palma as Secretary of the "International Committee for the Defense of Ricardo Flores Magón and Librado Rivera," the circular had been mailed to an address in Lima, Peru. In it, the committee declared that "to buy justice, money is necessary. In this system nothing can be done without money." Their appeal contained the prediction that both Flores Magón and Rivera would face twenty-five years in prison. In the same envelope, an appeal from María, dated June 24, 1918, described wartime conditions as almost total submission to "Mrs. Authority," and claimed that even "so-called radicals" were afraid to talk because of the delicate nature of the times. María rhetorically placed her trust in "the rabble in whom I hope and confide for the liberty of the people of the globe," and signed the letter "Yours and the Anarchy's." Another letter—this one addressed to Callao, Peru—contained the same material. Two more envelopes addressed to Cuba completed the basis of the first count.[7]

The second count charged that at a time of war with Imperial Germany, the defendants had used disloyal, scurrilous, and abusive language in reference to the United States' form of government, its flag, and its military so as to bring them into disrepute, contempt, and scorn. The language of the manifesto of March 6 noted in the first count, allegedly supported the charge. Grounds for the third count, also based on the depositing in the mails copies of *Regeneración* containing the manifesto, sustained an Espionage Act violation.[8]

Sakharam G. Pandit, who defended María Flores Magón, contended that the alleged false reports and statements should be viewed as rhetorically phrased matters of opinion.[9] Pandit also told the court that María did not want to be tried with Nicholas Senn Zogg because she held his reputation to be malodorous—an indication of another split in the rapidly thinning ranks of the PLM. Judge Oscar A. Trippet, who had presided over Ricardo's 1916 trial, declined the request on the advice of the Assistant United States Attorney, W. F. Palmer.[10] Subsequently, María obtained her release on $5,000 bail, pledged by Reuben T. Forrester and Thomas Strain, on November 13, 1918, just two days after the signing of the armistice that ended the war.[11] Raúl Palma, held on $500 bail, got out of jail a day earlier. Mrs. Aurelia J. Corker and A. E. Press supplied the bail.[12]

Long delayed, the case never reached court. John R. O'Connor, the U.S. Attorney in Los Angeles, recommended to the Justice Department that it be dropped. Palma had shown himself not to be a fugitive, Zogg was serving a twenty-year federal sentence already, Zavala had fled, and Ricardo and Enrique Flores Magón, and Librado Rivera—who appeared to be the "brains" of the PLM—were all serving prison terms. Moreover, because of the long delay and changing public sentiment, O'Connor expressed doubts that a conviction could be obtained.[13] Obviously, the federal government itself had lost interest in the case and what remained of the PLM.

7

"Here Lies a Dreamer":
Leavenworth Federal Penitentiary, 1922

Sentenced once again to the federal penitentiary at McNeil Island, Washington, Ricardo Flores Magón never regained his freedom. Well into middle age, and aware that a twenty-one year sentence constituted a life term, Flores Magón endured a very painful self-evaluation. To make certain that the formerly strident revolutionary would have sufficient time for reflection and to ensure that he could never again unsettle federal authorities, Assistant United States Attorney W. F. Palmer advised the Federal Board of Parole not to release Flores Magón until he accepted the principle that change in the United States occurred through "the ballot and not the bullet." Palmer perceived Flores Magón as a dangerous man who played upon the "ignorance and stupidity of the Mexican population."[1] In a socially negative sense, Palmer recognized Flores Magón's efforts on behalf of Mexican-American workers throughout the Southwest, and feared the political potential of his movement.

The Justice Department considered Flores Magón an internal security problem, both as an anarchist dedicated to the destruction of the state and as a dangerous influence on Mexicans, and those of Mexican extraction living in the United States. The latter objection took precedence because of the unusual influx of Mexican labor necessitated by World War I. The law restricting contract labor had been suspended so that low-paid Mexican workers could be utilized, and, as the number of Mexicans in the West and Southwest increased, so did their importance.

Nevertheless, in spite of the need for Mexican workers,

employers could not be relied upon to deal fairly with them. For example, Consul General Teódulo Beltrán reported that workers employed by the Spreckles Sugar Company endured treatment that rivaled what had formerly been inflicted on Porfirian peons. Irregular pay and hours, inadequate housing, and the use of armed guards resulted in what the consul called near-slavery conditions.[2] Worker resentment constituted a potentially explosive situation. Although often unskilled and illiterate, many Mexicans had heard of Ricardo Flores Magón and associated him with a concern for the well-being of peasants and workers. Flores Magón, as Palmer sensed, would have attempted to enlist such workers in the struggle. His anarchism and his opposition to social and economic exploitation made him a potential menace to production dependent on Spanish-speaking labor in California and other areas of the country.[3]

Mexican and Mexican-American labor, hampered by lack of effective leadership as well as the problem of organizing in a hostile cultural environment, nevertheless had made some progress. Militant miners forced a compromise solution in the 1915 Arizona strike that affected the Clifton, Morenci, and Metcalf operations. Mexican miners made up nearly eighty percent of the work force in that area, and they used the power of innumerable "striketos" to control working conditions.[4] Then, in 1919, Mexican-Americans joined an unsuccessful strike against the Los Angeles Railway and Pacific Electric. Agricultural workers also attempted to use strikes to achieve basic economic objectives. Counter-violence, jailing, and deportations barely controlled the situation. Under such circumstances, it is easy to understand the alarm with which officials viewed Flores Magón and his potential activities if he regained his freedom.[5]

At McNeil Island, Ricardo's already-fragile health deteriorated significantly. Overcome by depression, he spent his time trying to escape into a mind crippled by a lack of hope.[6] His wife, María, deeply concerned for her husband's health, appealed for financial aid to enable Flores Magón to receive better medical attention than that normally accorded the inmates at McNeil.[7] According to María, he suffered greatly from chronic diabetes. In a letter to his lawyer requesting a transfer to Leavenworth, Kansas, Flores Magón himself complained of an ulcerated foot and rheumatism. He described the effect of his rapidly failing eyesight as the sensation of peering through a fog.[8] A urinanalysis made at McNeil indicated an extremely high sugar content, and as a result, Flores Magón was placed on a strict diet until his transfer to Leavenworth at the end of 1919. Librado Rivera, whom María claimed also suffered from poor health, soon followed him to Kansas. Unfortunately, at Leavenworth, Flores Magón's health problems worsened. The available medical attention, adequate for minor ailments and injuries, appears to have been unsatisfactory for serious illnesses. Rivera insisted that Flores Magón had not received adequate consideration from medical officials at the penitentiary.[9]

Nevertheless, prison authorities did not completely disregard Flores Magón's health needs. Several months prior to his death, after he began coughing up blood, he received an examination and laboratory tests were conducted. Unfortunately, the medical response remained perfunctory. Flores Magón correctly noted that the government viewed his condition in a most impersonal way. After all, federal officials were part of a "huge machine" without a heart, nerves, or conscience. He acutely felt the prison bureaucracy's lack of personal concern: to the authorities, he was only a number, a statistic, another possible candidate for a prison burial. Caught in a web of disinterested procedure, the anarchist in him registered the dehumanization caused by that alleged social instrument—the state.[10]

His failing health worried his supporters. Kate Crane Gartz, a wealthy Southern California socialist and heiress to the Crane industrial fortune, whose brother, Charles R. Crane, personally knew President Woodrow Wilson and his daughter, wrote a letter to Margaret Wilson appealing for the release of the ailing Flores Magón. Crane Gartz also described María as living in "abject squalor," selflessly concerned over her husband's health, while she tried to recover her own after being released from Los Angeles County jail. Crane Gartz begged Wilson's daughter to convince the President that harsh repression, as exemplified by Flores Magón's experience, could end only in revolution.[11]

After 1920, support for Flores Magón and pressure for his release came from two separate sources. Once the war ended, demands for the release of political prisoners, including Eugene V. Debs, being held at the federal penitentiary in Atlanta, Georgia, mounted. As a victim of the Espionage Act, Ricardo Flores Magón clearly fell into the category of a poltical prisoner. Moreover, events in Mexico reached the point where his past activities could be utilized for political purposes by various political groups. President Alvaro Obregón, a pragmatist rather than an idealist, had begun already to create special interest groups to support his regime, including the urban laboring class as well as agrarian groups. Both constituencies stood for important philosophical concepts that Flores Magón had fought for throughout his career. Thus, Antonio Díaz Soto y Gama, an early supporter of the PLM, who had chosen to take an active role in revolutionary events and to support political solutions, convinced the Mexican congress to vote for providing Flores Magón with a government pension. Although obviously touched by the sympathy and recognition implied by the act, Flores Magón decided that if he had failed in everything else, he had at least never betrayed his principles—virtually the only thing he had left.[12] Ricardo suggested that while as an anarchist, he could not accept money from the state, he would accept money "with pleasure, even pride" directly from the workers.[13]

From Leavenworth, Flores Magón wrote a series of philosophical letters. To his friends, he reflected on his personal despair, yet resisted the temptation to become bitter and cynical about the people's ability to accept anarchist political formulas. His correspondence contains the thoughts of a man conscious of the approaching end of life. He sought to reassure himself that his past activities were in accord with those lofty ideals that occasionally, in more active periods of life, become blurred. If he had once lashed out at the fainthearted or disillusioned colleagues and enemies in a harsh fashion, Flores Magón, nearing his death, was now prepared to concede their sincerity. He viewed himself not as an intellectual who actively defined problems and demanded their resolution, but as a dreamer. He observed that even while practical men and women may laugh at dreamers, they are the "true dynamic force that pushes the world forward." At the same time, he acknowledged that he had been busy "seeding, seeding," without hope of an immediate harvest.[14] He hoped that the seeds planted during a lifetime of struggle would determine eventually the future shape of the fruit.

Inside Leavenworth, Flores Magón worked in the prison library along with Taraknath Das, an East Indian nationalist, and Brent Dow Allinson, a conscientious objector from Chicago. According to Ralph Chaplin, the IWW poet and fellow inmate, Flores Magón worked behind a desk piled high with books, looking anything but like the man reputed to be among the most dangerous in the institution. Enrique, also confined to Leavenworth—where he worked on the rock pile—impressed observers as more of a typical "insurrecto" than his brother. Librado Rivera worked in the prison print shop, where he surreptitiously printed Mexican revolutionary poems translated by Chaplin. Rivera became the confidant of Mexican-American and Mexican prisoners, while Flores Magón remained more aloof, revered as the highest of idealists.[15] Flores Magón worked with Chaplin on translations of Práxedis Guererro's revolutionary poems, professing great admiration for the young poet who had died during the battle of Janos, Chihuahua, in one of the PLM's attempts to topple Porfirio Díaz.[16]

Meanwhile, New York attorney Harry Weinberger led a legal effort to free Flores Magón. Weinberger specialized in cases involving freedom of the press and individual liberties, often without compensation.[17] He had successfully defended Emma Goldman against a second attempt to imprison her for distributing birth-control information, and had represented both Emma and Alexander Berkman in numerous other legal actions. In the case of Ricardo Flores Magón, it is doubtful that he received even his basic expenses. Ironically, Flores Magón suffered the same disability that he faced in his other judicial battles by accepting legal assistance from any quarter. His attorney could not function ideally as a third party pleading the case of a client. Instead, he himself became prey to the emotional reaction against radicals. In each instance, the government manipulated public sentiment itself, violating the spirit of the United States Constitution and the laws protecting individual liberties. In Weinberger's case, the reaction was particularly strong: In an effort to free Goldman and Berkman from their convictions of conspiracy to obstruct military induction, he had once argued before the Supreme Court against the constitutionality of the draft. As a result, neither the government nor the public had the slightest doubt on which side he stood. To have him pleading for Flores Magón's release merely confirmed the connection between the Mexican anarchist and American radical elements.[18] Harry Weinberger, apparently aware of the problem, wrote President Harding on April 25, 1921, to say, "I am pleading in the matter a human case and not a law case, as I was not the attorney for Mr. Magón who was tried in the West."[19]

The Justice Department did not have to resort to complex legal maneuvers to keep Flores Magón imprisoned. When Weinberger pressed the matter of a pardon, he would be informed that Ricardo had not requested one, and, therefore, could not be considered for clemency. To beg for a pardon would have been the ultimate humiliation for Flores Magón. Federal officials, on the other hand, demanded a show of repentance from their political prisoners; in effect, an admission of guilt and a reassurance that the government had acted correctly. This official attitude toward political prisoners is clearly evident in Attorney General Palmer's arguments in the Eugene V. Debs case. In correspondence with President Wilson, Palmer indicated that he felt a ten-year sentence to be too harsh—yet advised against freeing Debs because he had been in jail only a few months and, perhaps, even more importantly, "is absolutely unrepentant."[20]

Later, when referring to Flores Magón, Attorney General

Harry M. Daugherty complained that "he in no manner evinces any evidence of repentance."[21] Evidently, a contrite Flores Magón, willing to renounce anarchism and publicly acknowledge his guilt by requesting a pardon, would have been released. In spite of failing health and near-blindness, Ricardo wrote to his old friend Nicolás Bernal that he could not pay the price demanded—that of his honor. He suggested a fitting epitaph: "Here lies a dreamer." Flores Magón admitted that his enemies might claim "Here lies a madman," but no one could say, "Here lies a coward and a traitor to his ideas."[22] To the end, Ricardo Flores Magón refused to betray his ideals in exchange for freedom. Instead, he chose to reaffirm his anarchism and abhorrence of private property.

His personal belief that he would die in prison reflected an accurate assessment of his health. Ricardo's constant complaints about his health alarmed his family and friends. They continually pressured the Justice Department for better treatment and outside medical evaluations. The last independent medical examination conducted a little more than a month before his death concluded that his general physical condition remained good. Flores Magón, upon receiving a copy from attorney Harry Weinberger, sarcastically refuted the conclusions and maintained he was "sick and very sick." His self-diagnosis was dated November 5—he would be dead sixteen days later. Warden W. T. Biddle explained the discrepancy between Ricardo's health claims and those of medical specialists as an attempt by Flores Magón, "a well-educated, cunning Mexican," to stir things up. In the end the patient knew better. Indeed, Ralph Chaplin observed that his condition seemed to deteriorate day by day.[23] On November 21, 1922, at the age of forty-nine, Flores Magón died. A heartbroken Librado Rivera insisted that he had been murdered. There were, in fact, unexplained marks on his neck and his features had contorted as if he had struggled.[24] Although he had complained frequently of diabetes, it is not clear whether his condition had ever been medically confirmed. In any case, his death appears to have been consistent with the effects of diabetes. Medical research indicates that approximately half the people stricken with heart attacks between the ages of thirty and fifty suffer from the disease. His impending blindness also can be attributed to diabetes. Whatever the contributing factors, the immediate cause of death appears to have been a heart attack.[25]

Following so extended a period of failing health, Flores Magón's death should not have come as a surprise. Nevertheless, his fellow inmate friends reacted bitterly.[26] Eugene V. Debs charged that the prison death amounted to execution by the United States Department of Justice. With his own health adversely affected by imprisonment, Debs compared Flores Magón with the "Man of Galilee"—a selfless man who espoused the cause of the poor only to become a victim of the incredible savagery of the government. The old socialist proposed that Flores Magón's epitaph might well be "This hero, this martyr of humanity was put to death by slow torture by the government of the United States."[27]

Kate Crane Gartz sent a strongly worded telegram to President Warren G. Harding in which she predicted that Flores Magón's name would live on even while the names of his torturers already had died.[28] The *Baltimore Sun* commented that, in reality, Flores Magón never posed a threat to American security, especially since "the articles in the little paper which he published in Los Angeles were in the Spanish tongue and as little likely to discourage recruiting as a Dutch edition of the New Testament."[29] Rudy Herman bitterly noted that the working people for whom Flores Magón had given his life did not seem to realize that he ever lived. They just continued to prattle aimlessly about "the Mahoney Case—the latest about Jack Dempsey—whether 'flappers' should be censured for smoking cigarettes—Fatty Arbuckle's latest scandal—their favorite movie star—the 'prettiest' waitress in the city—Babe Ruth's 'marvelous' playing—ad nauseam!"[30] A touching personal tribute came from Alexander Berkman, who noted that, "Ricardo was a splendid man and a devoted comrade."[31]

In memory of the man they respected, sympathizers held a "free speech and amnesty" meeting in Washington, D.C. The event attracted wide support and called for the release of all wartime political prisoners. Among those listed in support were members of Congress, much to the horror of Congressman Walter F. Lineberger of California, who insisted on recording his opinion that Flores Magón, as an anarchist, had posed an actual threat to the United States. Lineberger asserted that Ricardo tried to dissuade Mexican-Americans from serving in the army and, moreover, had urged them to return to Mexico, join the Germans, and recover the lost provinces of California, Texas, New Mexico, and Arizona.[32] In Los Angeles, the *Times* observed that Ricardo Flores Magón's final imprisonment resulted from his efforts to incite Southern California's large Mexican population against the war. The newspaper noted that for a time, the authorities viewed the Flores Magón brothers as "among the most dangerous in Los Angeles."[33]

In Mexico, Antonio Díaz Soto y Gama rose to his feet on the floor of the senate to pronounce Ricardo Flores Magón the "precursor of the revolution, its true author, the intellectual author of the Mexican revolution" who had now closed his life as he had opened it, "always a rebel, always unbending." Díaz Soto y Gama suggested that it had been only appropriate that the United States government refused to concede Flores Magón his liberty, for in that refusal, it had freed him to die for his principles and thereby to close a tragic but inspiring drama."[34] His comments conveniently failed to note that the Mexican government had not pressed energetically for the release of its now-dead hero. In reality, President Obregón's revolutionary pragmatism was well on the way to achieving the social and political stability that eventually evolved into the "institutionalized revolution." Such a philosophy sharply conflicted with Flores Magón's idealism. The state, whether on one side of the border or the other, preferred a silent Flores Magón. In prison or in death, he could not be the tireless agitator or the anarchist social critic who attacked both governments.

Many chose to overlook the basic and unrelenting hostility between anarchism and the state, and believed that Mexican government efforts to free the imprisoned man were

sincere. Indeed, Obregón had been pressured by state legis-
lators, powerful workers' organizations, as well as by the
Mexican Communist Party and the Young Communist League
to secure Flores Magón's release. To underscore their demands, various groups staged work stoppages in support
of their captive hero.[35] On May Day, members of the militant *Confederación General de Trabajadores* demonstrated in
front of the United States Embassy in Mexico City to demand
Ricardo Flores Magón's release and to condemn American
imperialism.[36] In Veracruz, an eerily silent demonstration un-
nerved the American consul. Rumors circulated about boy-
cotts of all American ships by stevedores and of American
products.[37] Labor organizations exerted unwelcome pressure
on both American diplomatic representatives and on the
Obregón government. An extremely talented if somewhat
cynical politician, General Obregón realized that the return
of Flores Magón might provide his enemies with a revolutionary symbol around which to rally. Such an eventuality would
have complicated efforts to consolidate power.[38]

Other concerns preoccupied Obregón. By late 1920, the
end of wartime economic expansion in the United States
caused an abrupt decline in the demand for Mexican labor.
By the beginning of 1922, some 20,000 workers and their
families had been stranded in the United States, and were on
the verge of starvation. As a result, a hard-pressed Mexican
government spent more than a million dollars before the crisis
abated. Repatriated workers, however, found it difficult to
find employment in their homeland, and consequently, by
the middle of 1922, emigration picked up once again.[39] President Obregón faced a potentially dangerous political and social problem posed by unemployed Mexican workers, whether
in Mexico or across the border. Repatriated workers returned
to Mexico with an expanded political awareness that made
them much more critical of the failings of the Mexican government and the country's inability to employ its people.[40] In an
effort to head off political problems and avoid socioeconomic
disaster, Mexican officials hoped for a formal agreement with
American employers or the United States government. In

order to confront pressing economic concerns, Obregón desperately needed American recognition and normalization of diplomatic relations. He hesitated to complicate political matters by demanding the release of Flores Magón. The fact that the United States appeared excessively concerned with Mexican radicalism provided an added reason for Obregón's reluctance to push aggressively for the release of an anarchist. A massive propaganda campaign, aimed at persuading U.S. business and political leaders that Obregón deserved diplomatic recognition, presented the President as a reasonable and practical businessman. The Mexican Ministry of Foreign Affairs reportedly spent close to $2 million on such efforts. A series of paid excursions to Mexico convinced many businessmen and politicians that he desired sincerely normal commercial and political relations.[41] Under such circumstances, Ricardo Flores Magón's release appeared relatively unimportant. In fact, the entire affair presented an unwelcome problem for a government attempting to placate internal radical elements even as it pressed the United States for recognition.

Ironically, as Ricardo languished in prison the Obregón government made an ostentatious fuss over Mother Jones, who had been invited to address the Pan-American Federation of Labor's convention in Mexico City in January of 1921. As a guest of the Mexican government she arrived on a special train after frequent stops along the way for worker delegations to present her with flowers. The newspaper *Excelsior,* referring to her as "Madre Juanita," noted the assistance she had given Mexican revolutionaries, including Ricardo Flores Magón. Artfully the article omitted the fact she had broken with the PLM in 1911, instead noting that General Antonio I. Villarreal, a former associate of Flores Magón and now a high official, had made a special trip to New York to present her with a gold watch in gratitude. Madre Juanita had been folded gently into the revolutionary myth being elaborated by the Mexican government. In the capital she toured around in a chauffeured official car. The presence of both Mother Jones and Samuel Gompers of the AFL offered a public relation's bonanza. The Obregón government appeared both radical and responsible at the same time.[42] In a letter he wrote to the influential *New Republic* and through which he intended to marshal the liberal intelligentsia behind the Flores Magón campaign, Harry Weinberger indicated that the Mexican ambassador had formally requested Ricardo's release. Still, the lawyer continued, the American government did not seem in any hurry to comply.[43] Several months before Flores Magón's death, Kate Crane Gartz queried Attorney General Daugherty as to why the prisoner had not been released after Mexico requested such action. She speculated as to what reaction there might have been, had the United States demanded the return of a political prisoner held in a Mexican jail.[44] Crane Gartz and Weinberger both failed to appreciate the ambivalent attitude of the Mexican government, which limited the degree of pressure brought to bear on Washington.

The Mexican Embassy in Washington, D.C., based its half-hearted request for Flores Magón's release on the grounds that his health appeared to be extremely poor. Moreover, the embassy maintained that his offense was political, not criminal. In response, the U.S. Department of State informed the Mexican government that President Warren G. Harding had reviewed the case personally without finding any justification for the release of a dangerous anarchist with a history of repeated offenses. The State Department further declared that the Mexican note contained nothing to justify any change in the official attitude toward Flores Magón or Librado Rivera.[45] Obviously, the diplomatic stakes could have been raised by the Mexican government if it so desired.

Flores Magón's body would not be consigned to Peckerwood Ridge, Leavenworth's cemetery, thanks to the compassion of Kate Crane Gartz. Hundreds of mourners viewed their dead hero at the Breese Brothers Mortuary on South Figueroa Street when his corpse returned to Los Angeles.[46] Plans to cremate the body changed when it became evident that many of his former sympathizers wanted a symbolic return of the political exile to the country of his birth. Later, the corpse was placed in a vault at Evergreen Cemetery in East Los Angeles until the details could be worked out. María Flores Magón refused to permit the Mexican government to transport her husband's remains, but accepted the offer of Mexican railway workers to transport the body back to Mexico.

On January 5, 1923, Ricardo Flores Magón recrossed the frontier at El Paso, Texas, leaving the country he had entered so many years before. Honored in death as he could never have been in life, he would eventually be enshrined in the Rotunda of Illustrious Men at Mexico City's Dolores Cemetery. Thus, Flores Magón became part of the nationalistic myth of the "institutionalized Mexican revolution"—an anarchist building block for the structure of the state. Perhaps he should have remained in Evergreen Cemetery, close to the scene of his labors and surrounded by the Mexican-American working-class barrio of East Los Angeles.

8

The Limits of Freedom

Ricardo Flores Magón's place in Mexican history rests on his early call to arms against the Porfirio Díaz regime. The PLM defined the political and social abuses that the Mexican revolution would later pledge to remedy. As the designated intellectual progenitor of the revolution, Flores Magón's ideas could be successfully, but very selectively, plundered to provide a social platform for postrevolutionary politicians. Not surprisingly, Flores Magón's image as a liberal survives. But his anarchism, with its total opposition to the state, has been converted into an odd form of emotional revolutionary fervor devoid of political content. By emphasizing certain ideas and downplaying others, Flores Magón's anarchism is made subservient to a state that boasts of caging revolutionary energy within an "institutionalized revolution."[1]

Flores Magón's contribution to Mexican political mythology is quite different from his historical role. In contrast, his place in the history of American radicalism has escaped distortion for state purposes, yet at the same time, the importance of his long struggle among Mexican-Americans and Mexicans working in the United States and his political influence upon them has been almost totally ignored.

Success or failure is relative when assessing an individual's importance in radical politics in the United States. Radicalism subjected to virtually unremitting pressure from industrialists and the state could not succeed. The socialists alone enjoyed limited but important victories. Yet even their failure looms larger than success. Anarchism in the United States entered a new and foreboding stage with the Haymarket executions. The efforts of Emma Goldman, Alexander Berkman, and a sizable group of brilliant intellectuals of many nationalities were no match for an increasingly aroused and hostile state. It was not a question of the number of adherents. Membership in various anarchist organizations continued to swell following the Haymarket affair, particularly among Italian immigrants.[2] Nevertheless the survival of anarchism became problematic as the state began the process of mustering public opinion as well as repressive forces against the perceived threat to its existence. It was a bitter and protracted process, but one that eventually destroyed anarchism as a political factor in American life. Within this dismal matrix, one must evaluate Flores Magón's importance not by his failures, but by the recognition accorded him by the Left and the government of the United States. Prince Peter Kropotkin, one of the major theoreticians of anarchist thought, acknowledged the importance of Flores Magón's efforts, as did Alexander Berkman, Emma Goldman, and Voltairine de Cleyre. They willingly devoted their time and used their influence on behalf of the PLM. Eugene V. Debs, the giant of American socialism, along with Samuel Gompers of the AFL, recognized the validity of Flores Magón's social criticism. Elizabeth Gurley Flynn, not one to forgive even momentary faintheartedness, characterized the Flores Magón brothers as "heroic fighters."[3] A series of American presidents became familiar with his name and activities as did the attorneys general of the era.

Ricardo Flores Magón recognized, perhaps more than most radicals of the times, the interdependence of Mexican and American labor. His "Manifesto to the Workers of the United States" set forth logical arguments for working-class cooperation that are still applicable. The struggle of the Mexican worker against hunger and poverty directly involved the American laborer, whose ability to demand higher wages and better working conditions could be undermined by the mass movement of Mexican immigrants into the United States. As César Chavez and the United Farm Workers Union discovered, poverty-driven, illegal immigrants threatened attempts to organize the farm factories of the Southwest effectively.[4] Like Flores Magón, who warned that suffering across the border should not be ignored, the United Farm Workers Union has found that limited solutions, such as restrictive immigration policies that overlook social realities, have little impact. Thus, the problems pointed out by Ricardo Flores Magón remain. The PLM predicted the flight of American industry into low-wage areas as well as the result—unemployed northern workers venting their anger against members of the same economic class who work at exploitive wage rates south of the border. The PLM called for an interregional approach that is even more valid from a socioeconomic standpoint for both Mexico and the United States today than it was then.[5]

Flores Magón's anarchist perspective moved beyond the Mexican scene. In keeping with the actions of an immigrant the PLM leader had, by the very act of adjusting to a new culture, been shocked into an appreciation of a wider horizon. While he never lost sight of his hopes for his native land, Flores Magón saw Mexico's role in light of an overall world pattern. As a Mexican, he hoped that his country would help show the way for the rest of the world, including the United States. The continued existence of communal land in Mexico, despite a century of social and economic oppression by a series of governments, seemed to be proof of the viability of at least a primitive anarchism. In that sense, Mexico preserved the germ of regeneration that the rest of the world could draw upon.[6]

Flores Magón's failure to return to his native land is partially explained by the internationalization of his perspective. The barricades to be mounted against the capitalist system, and its instrument the state, existed worldwide and the battle itself had to be seen in such terms. While the struggle involved a Mexico dominated by foreign capital the front line was everywhere including the United States. Moreover, he believed that an important part of his efforts had to be devoted to heading off intervention by the American government in the Mexican revolution as it unfolded—a task better carried out in the United States itself. The implied charge that Flores Magón, because of his unwillingness to lead personally the PLM attacks on the border, was a physical coward appears groundless. Leadership within an anarchist framework did not involve the elaboration of a disciplined command structure with one individual at its head, rather it constituted a task of awakening the workers to their true interests; at that point, the capitalist system, without anyone left to carry out its order, would collapse. Lecturing, writing, agitation—in short, the task of education—took precedence over all other activities. It should be noted also that a coward would not have exposed himself to repeated imprisonment. Jails and federal penitentiaries caused him despair, depression, frustration, and eventually contributed to breaking his health. It may be argued, however, that Flores Magón made many mistakes. If the PLM had allied itself with other Mexican revolutionary groups, undoubtedly Ricardo's influence on the course of the Mexican revolution would have been greater. Such alliances could only have been carried forward by returning to his native land. It would also have required a degree of ideological opportunism. The PLM's headquarters in the United States should have been established closer to major border cities. A base in San Antonio, Texas, would have enabled Flores Magón to stay in better contact with Mexican supporters. Madero, in comparison, understood that the entryway to Mexico lay along the border with Texas, not the marginal frontier region in California. The most important mistake remains the PLM's failure to publicly convey its anarchistic program prior to 1911. Had it been announced in 1906 success might have continued to elude Flores Magón, but his impact on the social and political structure of postrevolutionary Mexico would have been significant and substantive rather than mythological.

By the time of his final imprisonment, Flores Magón had become much more than the provincial revolutionary. No other major political figure involved in the Mexican revolution thought in global terms. Emiliano Zapata, Francisco Villa, Venustiano Carranza, Alvaro Obregón, and others could not claim to be concerned with a worldwide revolutionary movement. Only the anarchistic *Casa del Obrero Mundial* shared such an encompassing view. Unfortunately, the

Casa fell victim to manipulating politicians and narrow political considerations. In the end, only Flores Magón survived
as an advocate of a universal approach. *Regeneración* deliber-
ately addressed universal problems with wide applications
outside the narrow limits of a single country. Flores Magón's
opposition to conscription and World War I stemmed not
from Mexican considerations, but from his philosophical position that capitalist-controlled governments merely sought to
convert "industrial slaves" into cannon fodder. Clearly Flores
Magón did not ignore the environment in which he labored.
He chose not to remain a transient political exile and concentrate only on those questions which concerned his native
land. If he had, his experience with the American judicial system would have been quite different. Like many other immigrants, the ragged band of PLM members that crossed into
Laredo in 1904 arrived in the United States with many pre-
conceived notions about liberty and were unaware that free
speech existed more as a rhetorical ideal than an established
fact. Flores Magón's anarchism—which matured after he became established in the United States—could only have been
strengthened by his loss of faith in the protection theoretically
offered under the Constitution of the United States.

Flores Magón's anarchist view of the state reflected the
belief that the state legalized, as well as perpetuated, social
inequities. It therefore had to be viewed as a class weapon
directed consciously against the masses. Those in power facilitated class repression and arranged the judicial process to
make it work to their benefit. In Flores Magón's view, the
protection of the sanctity of private property became the
building block of class privilege, and ultimately, the state's
sole objective. Ricardo Flores Magón's experience with the
judicial system served to confirm his views. Indeed, his open
hostility to the state forced the government to protect itself,
despite the fact that the danger was always more philosophical than real.

Although he attempted to rally its support for a worldwide
revolution including Mexico, Flores Magón never quite understood the nature of the American Left. The PLM tapped

a wide spectrum of left-wing support from liberals, to socialists, Wobblies, and fellow anarchists. Ricardo Flores Magón did not insist on principle in his dealings with such supporters. The PLM, beleaguered by the American judiciary, accepted aid from any quarter. By manipulating external sources of support Ricardo in turn found himself used by those with a different agenda. In a number of instances who used whom is uncertain. The party became somewhat of a "pet cause" in left-wing circles. One has the uneasy feeling that Flores Magón missed becoming one of Mabel Dodge's New York salon oddities simply by the grace of geographical location.[7] In contrast, he allowed for no compromise over principles within the PLM's ranks. He also held fellow Mexican revolutionaries to an impossibly rigid standard that they inevitably failed to meet. A long list of former friends and colleagues became alienated. In fact, a number were driven out of the PLM. Flores Magón's single-minded attachment to his beliefs could not accommodate the failings of family or friends. Those who claim he made a natural martyr are supported by history. Indeed his personality may have been better suited for that role than for political success.

Flores Magón was a serious revolutionary despite the disappointments and failures. The United States government initially viewed him as a Mexican problem, but in the end, it considered him a danger to internal security and responded accordingly. Consequently, to protect itself, the state conducted blatantly political trials in 1916 and 1918. Even in the 1912 proceedings, which grew out of the PLM's invasion of Baja California, the government appeared more interested in controlling radicalism than attempting to uphold the neutrality laws. Ricardo Flores Magón impressed federal authorities to the point that they considered him to be part of the dangerous radical element that included the IWW, anarchists, and socialists. Leftist opposition to World War I and support of the 1917 Bolshevik revolution confirmed the government's belief that individuals, such as Flores Magón, jeopardized the very existence of capitalism and the state. Flores Magón's final penal sentence reflected the federal government's fear.

Public opinion supported blatantly rigged trials of anarchists. General acceptance of the notion that the threat required the setting aside of legal niceties made transparent travesties of justice possible. Violence, or the fear of it, legitimized state force. The fact that those on trial might not be guilty of the charges mattered little because they must be guilty of something equally as deserving of punishment. The execution of Nicola Sacco and Bartolomeo Vanzetti in 1927 provided the most tragic and shameful example of unrestrained public opinion and its manipulation to curb anarchism. Rather pathetically, Alice Stone Blackwell, who corresponded with Ricardo during his confinement in Leavenworth, wrote to Vanzetti concerning Flores Magón's struggle. Vanzetti in his response empathized, but also noted that Ricardo had died in "chains."[8]

As a victim of political persecution, Ricardo Flores Magón took part in one of the most important struggles of American democracy—the continuing, and far from won, battle to establish the principle of freedom of speech. Flores Magón's personal landmark in the struggle for free speech in the United States resulted from the 1916 case when he and his brother, Enrique, became the first individuals to be convicted under section 211 of the amended Federal Penal Code of 1910 that defined obscene nonmailable matter to be material that tended to incite arson, murder, or assassination. By declaring *Regeneración*'s editorials to be "vile and filthy," the government effectively suppressed freedom of speech under the guise of obscenity control. This was not a very laudable signpost on the way to full protection of first-amendment rights, yet certainly a significant one. Although politically dormant, this definition survives as part of the law more than a half century after Flores Magón's 1916 conviction.[9]

Flores Magón's experience with the American judicial system exemplifies a still unresolved legal, political, and libertarian issue: How far a state may go to protect itself against those that seek its destruction before it infringes on freedom of speech. Just as difficult to resolve is a corollary issue—when does revolutionary rhetoric become dangerous to the state and its social mandate to govern? Ricardo Flores Magón unquestionably worked for the destruction of the state. If the people had taken to the streets in response to his fiery phrases, he would have been delighted. Actually, Flores Magón failed to galvanize the working class into revolutionary action and posed little real danger to the government. Of course, historical judgment was a luxury unavailable to government officials charged with the immediate protection of the state. In essence, they took Flores Magón at his word and destroyed him.

The Flores Magón trials demonstrated the extent to which the judicial system responded to public opinion and the resultant political concerns. Judges as political appointees could not avoid an awareness of both public and official opinion. While charged with the objective application of the law they functioned within a politicized system with its attendant pressures and obligations. When the case before the court had important political implications the outcome depended in part on their own attitude and the extent of their social or political allegiances. In wartime, or other moments of perceived national crisis, including acute anarchist scares, impartial justice became difficult to achieve. In the PLM's case some judges did better than others. Judge Oscar A. Trippet (1916 trial), aware of the problem, contemplated resolving it by securing Ricardo's agreement to leave the country. Voluntary deportation, while frequently employed, avoided the issue. Judge Benjamin F. Bledsoe (1918 trial) on the other hand made no secret of his own opinions, brought them forward throughout the trial, and allowed them to determine the severity of the sentence. Anarchists, including the Flores Magón brothers, attacked the very notion of a state including its judicial arm. The object of their hostility, in the end, pronounced sentence.

Public attitudes could easily be orchestrated by those seeking to harness community sentiment in some fashion. In a representative political system a high level of hysteria can build up as a consequence of the interplay between an aroused community, only generally or weakly informed, and individuals supposedly dedicated to representing its interests. Constitutional guarantees, no matter how stated, remain subject to interpretation. The real or imagined circumstance of the country at a particular moment may force an interpretive decision that in different, calmer times would be inconceivable. Supreme Court Justice Oliver Wendell Holmes, who sat on the bench when the Espionage Act came under review, attempted to introduce a measure of objectivity through the elaboration of the "clear and present danger" standard. Over a period of time he modified the standard to support free speech unless an immediate check was necessary to save the country. For all its restraint Holmes's modified standard remains vulnerable to interpretive hysteria. When violence is perceived to be an integral part of a political movement the difficulty is compounded. Nevertheless, the criminalization of opinion in defense of the state is too primitive a response in a civilized society.[10]

The failure to define the nature of truly dangerous political conspiracy continues to threaten first-amendment rights and intimidates legitimate social criticism. Equally important, the lack of proper definition jeopardizes the theoretical right of the people to change the very nature and form of their government. Without rational and recognized guidelines the state is subject to wild and destructive swings from toleration and even extreme toleration in normal times to repression when faced by a political challenge, real or imagined.

Radicalism provides a useful if not readily appreciated sociopolitical function. Its extremist nature makes full implementation impossible. It posits an imaginative boundary placed well in advance of a reasonable social consensus. As a dying Ricardo Flores Magón correctly noted, he was a dreamer, a fate shared by all radicals even as they strive to be activists. Radicalism constitutes a rush of adrenalin to the body politic. It shocks, assaults the complacency of the governing elite, and opens the way to the formulation of a new political perspective. To destroy those that propose radical solutions is to drain the reservoirs of political innovation. The half-century between Flores Magón's birth and the year his corpse crossed the border proved to be crucial to the course of history of both Mexico and the United States. During that period American radicalism virtually was exterminated. As a result, in our time it survives only on the far philosophical fringes of American life. In Mexico the "institutionalized revolution" outmaneuvered the revolutionary dreamers. Today the political structure initially elaborated by President Alvaro Obregón stands in need of inspired renovation. A rich political legacy remains buried in history.

Appendix A

To the Workers of the United States, November 7, 1914

Brothers, Greetings!

It is known that the Mexican people have been in a state of armed revolution since four years ago, but very little is known about the nature of this gigantic movement, due to the fact that the capitalistic press tries to confuse through different means the minds of its readers, pretending that all the trouble there lies in useless quarrels of leaders, a conflict between spurious ambitions, whose only object is to strive for the Presidency of the republic. If to the surface of this tremendous conflict come the names of Villa, Carranza or any other personality, who, as shown by their actions, do not have any other objective than the acquisition of power. The truth is that those men are not the revolution, but mere military leaders that pretend to profit to their personal wishes out of the popular movement.

The Mexican people revolted in arms in November 1910, to conquer their economic freedom. In the minds of the rebelled workingmen there is no place for the idea of elevating this or that individual to the presidency of the republic, but of that wrenching the land, natural mother of all riches, out of the hands of the capitalist class and to make it the property of all and everyone of the inhabitants of the Mexican republic, men and women alike; and if the revolution is still on foot after four years have elapsed, it is because that just aspiration has been unable as yet to succeed in all the country.

That the Mexican revolution is essentially of an economical

[sic] nature at its bottom, is the opinion of the president of the United States, who instructed the American delegates to the peace conference at Niagara Falls not to accept any resolution that would not have as its basis the elimination of Huerta, and the establishment of a government in Mexico that would guarantee the solution of the agrarian problem, the president clearly expressing his opinion that there could not be peace in that country while the peons would not be in possession of the land.

This opinion is confirmed by the facts. Large territory extensions have been taken since the beginning of this revolution in different sections of the republic by proletarian multitudes that have placed them into cultivation, and have been gathering the crops for themselves. The property deeds have been burnt in the official files; the fences have been torn down; the warehouses and granaries have been left at the disposition of these revolutionary masses that understand that such expropriation is necessary, to subsist while the first crops are gathered; the houses have been left at the disposition of those who before had not a single clod of earth on which to lay their heads, and a marked tendency to socialize all the industries begins to be crystallized with the fact that the sugar factories and the distilleries of alcohols are being operated by the expropriating peons in the southern sections, where those industries predominate, and, in the fact, too, that some mines, wood mills and other enterprises are being operated by workingmen who have had the courage of recognizing that the machinery must be the property of the workingmen, and who, rifle in hand, have taken possession of it in the name of the revolution, which means in the name of justice.

The Mexican Liberal Party, by means of its oral and written propaganda and by its deeds, has played an important role in the class struggle that is being enacted in Mexico. This party is represented by a junta, at 2325 Ivanhoe Avenue, Los Angeles, Cal., formed by five members, Ricardo Flores Magón, Librado Rivera, Enrique Flores Magón, Antonio de P. Araujo and Anselmo L. Figueroa, and the official organ of this organization is *Regeneración*, written in Spanish and English.

Proved as it is that the Mexican revolutionary movement is of economic character, it is a duty of all class conscious workingmen to support with all their moral and material strength the workingmen who are spilling their blood to shake off the yoke of capitalism. The Mexican problem is not really a problem incumbent only to Mexico; it is a universal problem, it is the problem of hunger, the problem that the disinherited of all the world have to resolve under the penalty of living with their bodies bent down under the yoke of the master class. To deny solidarity to the Mexican workingmen who are struggling to conquer their economic freedom is to stand against the labor cause in general because the cause of the wage-slave against his master has no frontiers; it is not a national problem, but a universal conflict; it is the cause of all the disinherited of the world over, of everyone who has to work with his hands and his brains to bring his family a loaf of bread. If the economic revolution is crushed, the American workingmen will suffer the consequences, for an immigration of Mexican workingmen still greater than the one that has been taking place during the last ten or fifteen years, will take place, and the salaries in this country will be lower still. But that is not all; the crushed revolution means a victorious capitalism. The wealth of the magnates of American industry will flow into Mexico, to them, a field for all the adventurers and all the exploiters; the manufacturers of the United States would be transplanted to Mexico, that would become an ideal land for business because of the cheapness of salaries, and the American workingmen will find their factories and firms in this country closed down because it will be more profitable to their bosses to open their business where they will pay twenty-five to fifty cents a day for the same kind of work for which they would have to pay two or three dollars a day in this country. Then, you see, American workingmen, that it is not only because they are members of your own class and champions of the struggle of your class that you should help those in Mexico fighting for Land and Liberty, but for the fact, too, that they are laboring for your welfare while fighting for their own which comes to prove that the cause of the working class is but one, and that what affects the cause of the working class in one country, equally affects the working class in the rest of the countries of the world. That is why the workingmen of one country should consider himself closely united to the workingmen of all the other countries.

Keep in mind that the Mexican population of the southern states of the American union runs to the millions; keep in mind that the lands and the mines of Texas are being worked by Mexicans; that the fields in Louisiana and Mississippi are tilled by Mexicans; that the mines in Oklahoma and many others in Arizona, Nevada and Colorado are operated by Mexicans; that the great plantations in Colorado and California progress by the work of the Mexican; think that the workingmen laboring along the railroad lines are Mexicans and that Mexicans are the ones that keep running all the smelters scattered along the boundary line between this country and Mexico, and that numerous camps of Mexican workers are found in Wyoming, Iowa, Nebraska, Kansas, Missouri, Utah, Illinois and other states. Think, American proletarians what the pacific conquest of the Mexican toiler would mean to the rise of your salaries and to your complete emancipation.

To give a formidable impulse to this war against privilege and oppression money is needed most urgently. You have got it; give it to us! Our history of struggles and sacrifices for over twenty-two years place us above all suspicion. The best guarantee of our honesty is the twenty-two years that we have undergone in dungeons where tyranny would thrust its fangs in our throats to punish our loyalty and devotion to the interests of the working class, or in the clutches of poverty— that grim companion of all of us who would not sell our conscience nor betray our ideals.

Archimedes said: "Give me a basis [sic] and I will upturn the world."

We tell you: lend us solidarity and we will bury the capitalist system in Mexico.

Agitate incessantly. Show your brothers in chains the noble gesture of his Mexican brothers who has broken his chains and with them, handling them as a battering ram, batters down the walls of the castle where privilege and tyranny, shaking with fear, have sought safety, and remind them that their future depends on that rebel slave, that the interests of the working class are blended in such a way that it is impossible to look upon any aspect of the class struggle disdainfully without committing suicide. To act!

Send all correspondence and money to ANSELMO L. FIGUEROA, P.O. Box 1236, Los Angeles, Cal.

LAND AND LIBERTY

Los Angeles, Cal., November 7, 1914.

RICARDO FLORES MAGÓN.
ENRIQUE FLORES MAGÓN.
LIBRADO RIVERA.
ANTONIO DE P. ARAUJO.
ANSELMO L. FIGUEROA.

Appendix B

Address of Enrique Flores Magón in Federal Court, Los Angeles, June 22, 1916

On account of my brother's sickness, which prevents his addressing this Court, I shall speak in his behalf as well as my own. I am taking the opportunity given me of addressing the Court because I want to make clear the causes behind our prosecution, for it appears that Court procedure was designed to conceal the facts underlying such cases as this.

The records of this trial show that the Magón brothers were tried and convicted, but the records do not show that the case at bar here is the age-long fight of the downtrodden and the disinherited against the tyranny, the superstition and the oppression which overburdens mankind.

It is not merely the Magóns who are convicted in this Court, but all liberty and justice loving people; for we, the Magón brothers, have been convicted by the technicalities of man-made laws, for our activities in behalf of the emancipation of the downtrodden, particularly of the Mexican proletarians, and of the disinherited all over the world in general, as shown by our writings, which are a part of the record of this case.

With the Magóns you have convicted the world's redblooded men and women who are striving to halt the piracy and the oppression of the rapacious plutocracy and its natural allies, Authority and the Church. With us you have condemned all of the men and women who think and who feel the anguish and the sorrows of the dispossessed, the tortures of the oppressed, the wailing and the tears of the millions of human beings who have the misfortune of being born at a time when all of the means of life have been appropriated by the land-sharks and the money-grabbers of the millions of proletarians who are condemned at birth to a life of incessant toil and actual chattel slavery, without hope of any reward other than slow death from starvation and exposure.

After studying these conditions many men and women have come to the conclusion that the only way out of this slavery is the way we pointed out in our Manifesto of September 23rd, 1911. As we set forth in that document, we aim to establish the common ownership of the land, of the machinery and the means of production and distribution, for the common use and benefit of all human beings, so as to enable them to work and earn their own living and to enjoy the honest pleasures which nature intended for them.

These ideals are destructive to the present institutions, as properly remarked here by the prosecution and this Court, and are, therefore, antagonistic to man-made laws that uphold Capitalism, but this does not mean that they are not founded on sound principles of Justice and Freedom.

We are asked what we have to say why sentence should not be passed on us. This Court should not pass sentence on us, for it would mean to deny to us Mexican people the perfect right we have to revolt against the unbearable conditions that have kept us in slavery through long, long years; conditions under which we found ourselves stripped of all our belongings, our lands, our forests, our rivers, our mines and everything else that we once owned in common or individually since time immemorial. We saw all our belongings being taken from us by Porfirio Díaz by means of violence through his soldiery and legal machinery. Díaz robbed the Mexican people in order that he might grant concessions to the Otises, Hearsts, Rockefellers, Morgans, Guggenheims, Pearsons and other foreign interests. And these concessions were granted for a mere song in order to perpetuate the Díaz regime.

After we were dispossessed of our natural heritage, we found ourselves held in bondage, in real chattel-slavery, forced to work our own lands, lands that were now no longer ours; we were forced to work sixteen and eighteen hours a day for from $.18 to $.37 Mexican money, that is equal to from $.9 to $.18 American money. We were compelled to trade with the "tienda de raya," which is the same as the commissaries of your mining and lumber camps, where everything was sold to us at exorbitant prices. Under such conditions we gradually found ourselves in perpetual debt to our masters and without the liberty of moving from their domain. In case we succeeded in evading the vigilance of the hacienda bosses and escaped from our bondage, we were caught by the authorities and once more returned to slavery.

Whenever we went on strike for better conditions and wages, as in Rio Blanco and Cananea, we were shot down en masse by the trained murderers of Díaz, his soldiers, his policemen and rangers. If we still held a small piece of land that excited the greed of the authorities, the rich or the clergy, it was taken from us by hook or crook. They even resorted to cold-blooded murder.

Our freedom was trampled upon. Our speakers were arrested and shot in the dark of the night. Our papers were suppressed and the writers imprisoned, often vanishing from the face of the earth. Many of our brothers who still believed in the ballot met their death in front of the polls at the hands of the Díaz soldiers. Many of our brothers were sold for $200 per head to the slave drivers of Yucatán and the Valle Nacional. They were sold into actual slavery and there forced to work under such horrible conditions that their health was soon broken, and when they no longer could stand on their feet they were often buried alive in order to save bother and medical expenses. It was a common sight to see our brothers beaten to death for the slightest provocation.

We endured these conditions for thirty-six years, which proves that we are a peace-loving people. But we found ourselves so cornered and driven against the wall, that we finally had to revolt against damnable conditions in order to save ourselves and to gain Bread, Land and Liberty for All.

This was the cause and the source of the Social and Economic Revolution which has for over five years shaken

Mexico; the revolution of the downtrodden masses against their oppressors and exploiters; the revolution that chiefly aims to get control in common of the land and, thereby aims to free the Mexican people. These purposes and aspirations are set forth in condensed form in our battle cry of "Land and Liberty!"

We Mexicans are striving to get back the land, because we know that the land is the source of all social wealth and, therefore, that he who owns the land owns all and, hence, becomes economically free. A people who enjoy economic freedom are free socially and politically as well; that is to say, economic freedom is the mother of all freedom.

Against the outrageous conditions that I have here roughly outlined, we Mexicans revolted; and now two of us, Ricardo and myself, are facing sentence here for our activity in that rebellion and for striking to gain our political, social and economic emancipation.

We therefore think that, as a principle of justice, this Court should not impose a sentence on us; for such a sentence would mean a flat denial that the Mexican people have a right to fight their own battles and to fight them in their own way. Our revolutionary methods may not meet with the approval of the "peace at any price" gentlemen, but they have the sanction of Thomas Jefferson, who said: "We cannot expect to pass from Despotism to Liberty on a feather bed."

The institutions springing from private property are the source and cause of all slavery, vice and crime. It is on account of private property that a large majority of human beings are slaves; producing all the wealth, they go destitute. It is on account of private property, which deprives men and women of the just reward of their labor, that our women prostitute themselves, our children grow weak and consumptive in the mills of Capitalism, our men become drunkards, dope fiends, thieves, suicides, insane and murderers.

That is why we hate private property and fight for its abolition and strive to implant Communist anarchism wherein the land, the machinery and all the means of production and transportation shall be owned in common, so that all may have an equal chance for life, liberty and the pursuit of happiness; so that all being supplied in their needs and on an equal social, political and economic standing, ignorance, vice and crime shall vanish, naturally and automatically for their source, private property, will have been abolished forever.

We are opposed to the church for the reason heretofore given; it upholds the evil called private property and keeps submerged in ignorance and superstition the human mind.

We are opposed to government because it is the staunch upholder of private property and because government means imposition, tyranny, oppression and violence. We agree with Thomas Jefferson when he says: "History in general informs us how bad government is." While quoting Jefferson, I should like to remark that he was twice President of the United States, and, therefore, he knew what he was talking about. And on the 12th of this month, this court agreed with us when it said, "It is the duty of government to preserve itself." That means that government is not "of the people, by the people and for the people," but that it is in fact an institution alien to the people, and against whose interests it shall preserve itself. And we are duly grateful to this court for that acknowledgment.

Striving as we are through our revolutionary activities to gain justice, freedom, plenty and happiness for all human beings, we believe that, as a matter of justice this court has no right to impose a sentence on us. You may have the power, but you have not the right to do so.

The prosecution charged us with inciting to revolution in this country. The charge is baseless as well as illogical. Revolutions cannot be incited.

I have often compared the present conditions in this country with the conditions which confronted the Mexican people under the Díaz regime, and I have found them very similar in many instances. The American workingmen, as a whole, are often forced to work at wages on which no man can decently live, just as the Mexican peons were forced to do.

The lumber camps of Louisiana, the mines of Colorado and West Virginia and other places are practically the same as the hellholes of Yucatán and the Valle Nacional. Here also you have the "commissary" which is the counterpart of our "tienda de raya." Our massacres of Rio Blanco and Cananea have their parallel in Ludlow, Coeur D'Alene and West Virginia. The suppression of our papers by Díaz is similar to the suppression here of "The Woman Rebel," "Revolt," "The Alarm," "Voluntad," "The Blast," and finally, our "Regeneración." Free speech, free assemblage and free press, as well as freedom of thought, are dealt with in this country a la Porfirio Díaz.

On the other hand, you have here, as reported by the commission of industrial relations, 5 percent of the population owning 65 percent of the wealth, just as we had in Mexico. And as in Mexico, the multitude of producers are living either in pauperism or very close to actual want.

Here, too, you have your large landowners, and the number of your tenant farmers is ever increasing. American people, as the Mexican, are learning that the very earth under their feet has been taken away by the land-sharks and by huge land grants to special interests. Your mines and your forests are going the same way into the same hands that the mines and forests of Mexico went. The liberties of the American people have gradually been encroached upon just as they were in Mexico.

As like causes produce like results, it does not require a great deal of wisdom to see the trend of events of this country. Revolution is breeding, but it is coming from "above" and not from the workers, for it is only when the conditions of the proletariat become unbearable that they rise in revolt.

Unless present conditions change, you American people of the present generations will have to face the bloodiest revolution in the annals of history.

Jefferson, who was the anarchist of his time, and who is acknowledged as a great patriot and thinker, saw the necessity of revolution and justified its drastic measures. He said, "I hold that a little rebellion now and then is a good thing, and as necessary in the political world as storms in the physical." At another time he said, "The spirit of resistance is so valuable on certain occasions that I wish it always to be kept alive." And once more hear what Jefferson said: "Let these [the people] take arms. What signify a few lives in a century or two? The tree of liberty must be refreshed from time to time with the blood of patriots and tyrants. It is its natural manure."

In answer to the able argument for a new trial, made on the 12th of this month by our honest and courageous counsel, Mr. Ryckman, the Court said: "These men have no right to seek refuge in this country." We hold that we do have such right, not only as a principle of justice and civilization, but your constitution specifically grants us the right of asylum as political refugees.

Jefferson, Paine and Franklin, during the American revolution, not only acted as agents of the American rebels in France, but they actually secured the assistance of France in their revolt against England. From this we can see that one hundred and fifty years ago the French people recognized a principle of humanity which this court now denies us.

The court has spoken of us as aliens to this country and its people. The court is in error. We are aliens to no country, nor are we aliens to any people on earth. The world is our country and all men are our countrymen. It is true that, by birth, we are Mexicans, but our minds are not so narrow, our vision not so pitifully small as to regard as aliens or enemies those who have been born under other skies.

The court suggested that it would be more becoming for us to go to Mexico to shoulder a musket and fight for our rights. If the Mexican revolution were an attempt of one set of politicians to oust or overthrow another set of office-holders, then the court's suggestion would be very apt. The revolution in Mexico is, however, not a political but a social and economic revolution and it is necessary to educate people, to teach them the real causes of their misery and slavery, and to point out to them the way to freedom, fraternity and equality.

This is why our hands, instead of being armed with muskets are armed with pens; a weapon more formidable and far more feared by tyrants and exploiters. I believe that it was Emerson who said that "Whenever a thinker is turned loose, tyrants tremble." And it is because it is acknowledged that we are thinkers as well as fighters, that we have spent over seven years out of the twelve that we have been here in the jails and prisons of the land of the "free."

We are not asking the court for mercy; we are demanding justice. If, however, this court is to be actuated by man-made laws instead of fundamental justice and, therefore, insists on sending us to the penitentiary, you may do so without hesitation.

A penitentiary sentence to us will likely mean our graves, for we are both sick men. We alone know how our health has been undermined. We know that another penitentiary sentence, no matter how light it may be, will be a death sentence. We feel that we shall not come out of the penitentiary alive.

However, it does not matter to us personally; from the beginning of our struggle, twenty-four years ago, we dedicated our lives to the cause of freedom. Since that time we have suffered a long chain of persecution and conspiracy, of which this case is but another link, but we still hold to our original purpose of doing our duty to our fellowmen, no matter what the result to us personally.

History is watching us from her throne, and she is registering in her annals the social drama that is now being enacted in this court. We appeal to her with a clean conscience, and with our hearts normally beating and with our brains dreaming of a future society, wherein there will be happiness, freedom and justice for all mankind.

The court may choose between law and justice. If you send us to our graves and brand us once more with the stigma of felons, we are sure that history will reverse the sentence. She will mark indelibly the forehead of the Cain.

Let the Court speak! History watches!

Appendix C

U.S. Exhibit No. 12.

Indictment in the District Court of the United States in and for the Southern District of California, Southern Division

A true and correct translation of said manifesto is as follows, to-wit:

MANIFEST

The Assembly of Organization of the Mexican Liberal Party.

To the members of the Party, the Anarchists of the Whole World and the Workingmen in General.

Companions

The clock of history will soon point with its hands inexorable the instant producing death to this society already agonizing.

The death of the old society is close at hand, it will not delay much longer and only those will deny the fact whom its continuation interests; those that profit by the injustice in which it is based, those that see with horror the approach of the revolution for they know, that on the following day they will have to work side by side with their former slaves.

Everything indicates, with force of evidence that the death of the bourgeois society will come unexpectedly. The citizen with grim gaze looks at the policeman whom only yesterday he considered his protector and support; the assiduous reader of the bourgeois press shrugs the shoulders and drops with contempt the prostituted sheet in which appear the declarations of the chiefs of state; the working man goes on strike not taking into account that by his action he injures the country's interests, conscious now that the country is not his property but is the property of the rich; in the street are seen faces which clearly show the interior torment of discontent, and there are arms that appear agitated to construct barricades; murmurs in the saloons, in the theaters, in the streetcars, in each home, especially in our homes, in the homes of those below where is mourned the departure of a son called to war, or hearts oppressed and eyes moistened when thinking that tomorrow, perhaps today even, the boy who is the joy of the hut, the youngster who with his frankness and gentility wraps in splendor the gloomy existence of the parents in senescence will be by force torn from the bosom of the family to face, gun in hand, another youngster who like himself was the enchantment of his home and whom he does not hate and cannot hate for he even does not know him.

The flames of discontent revived by the blow of tyranny each time more enraged and cruel in every country and here and there everywhere and in all parts, the fists contract, the minds exalt, the hearts beat violently, and where they do not murmur they shout, all sighing for the moment in which the calloused hands during a hundred centuries of labor, they must drop the fecund tools, and grab the rifle which nervously awaits the caress of the hero.

Companions: The moment is solemn, it is the moment preceding the greatest political and social catastrophe that history registers; the insurrection of all people against existing conditions.

It will be surely a blind impulse of the masses which suffer, it will be without a doubt, the disorderly explosion of the fury restrained hardly by the revolver of the bailiff and the gallows of the hangman; it will be the overflow of all the indignation and all the sorrows and will produce the chaos, the chaos favorable to all who fish in turbid waters, chaos from which may sprout new oppressions and new tyrannies for such cases, regularly, the charlatan is the leader.

It falls to our lot, the intellectual, to prepare the popular mentality until the moment arrives, and while not preparing the insurrection, since insurrection is born of tyranny.

Prepare the people not only to await with serenity the grand events which we see glimmer, but to enable them to see and not let themselves be dragged along by those who want to induce them, now over a flowery road, toward identical slavery and a similar tyranny as today we suffer.

To gain that the unconscious rebelliousness may not forge with its own hands, a new chain that anew will enslave the people, it is precise, that all of us, all that do not believe in government, all that are convinced that government whichsoever its forms may be, and whoever may be the head, it is tyranny, because it is not an institution created for the protection of the weak, but to support the strong, we place ourselves at the height of circumstances, without fear propagate our holy anarchist ideal, the only just, the only human, the only true.

To not do it, is to betray knowingly the vague aspirations of the populace to a liberty without limits, unless it be the natural limits, that is, a liberty which does not endanger the conservation of the specie.

To not do it, is giving free hand to all those who desire to benefit merely their own personal ends through the sacrifice of the humble.

To not do it, is to affirm what our antagonists assure, that the time is still far away when our ideals will be adopted. Activity, activity and more activity is the demand of the moment.

Let every man and every woman who loves the anarchist ideal propagate with tenacity, with inflexibility, without heeding sneer not measuring dangers, and without taking on account the consequences.

Ready for action and the future will be for our Ideal.

Land and Liberty

Given in Los Angeles, State of California, United States of America, the 6th day of March 1918.

RICARDO FLORES MAGÓN.—LIBRADO RIVERA.

Note: Answers to this Manifest forward to Ricardo Flores
Magón. P. O. Box 1236. Los Angeles, Cal. U.S.A.

Contrary to the form of the Statute in such case made and
provided, and against the peace and dignity of the said
United States.

Notes

1: "THE FORCES OF LUCK"

1. Samuel Kaplan, *Combatimos la tirania: "Conversaciones con Enrique Flores Magón"* (Mexico, 1958), pp. 9–15.

2. Ethel Duffy Turner, *Ricardo Flores Magón y el Partido Liberal Mexicano* (Morelia, 1960), pp. 14–15.

3. Ricardo Flores Magón to unknown correspondent (July 9, 1922) in *Ricardo Flores Magón Epistolario revolucionario e intimo* (Mexico, 1925), 7: 44–45.

4. Kaplan, *Combatimos*, p. 25.

5. Ibid., pp. 19–21.

6. Turner, *Ricardo Flores Magón*, p. 25.

7. Ward Sloan Albro, III, "Ricardo Flores Magón and the Liberal Party: An Inquiry into the Origins of the Mexican Revolution of 1910 (Ph.D. diss., University of Arizona, 1967), p. 18.

8. Gonzáles Ramírez eloquently documents Flores Magón's losing battles with the courts before fleeing Mexico; imprisoned, May 1892 for one month, October 1901 for two-and-a-half months, in 1902 for nine months, April 1903 for eight months. Manuel González Ramírez, ed., *Epistolario y textos de Ricardo Flores Magón* (Mexico, 1964), p. 8.

9. Ricardo used *El Hijo del Ahuizote* after *Regeneración's* suppression. With his arrest followers kept it going by changing its name frequently. The government, determined to close every outlet, prohibited the circulation of any periodical carrying articles by Flores Magón under stiff penalties. Turner, *Ricardo Flores Magón*, pp. 59–60 and Norberto Aguirre, *Ricardo Flores Magón, síntesis biográfica* (Mexico, 1964), p. 13.

10. Some clues to Flores Magón's personality can be gleaned from his prison letters, however, because of the abnormal circumstances of imprisonment they must be used very carefully. A poignant collection is Paul Avrich, ed. "Prison Letters of Ricardo Flores Magón to Lilly Sarnoff," *International Review of Social History* (1977), pp. 379–422.

11. Diego Abad de Santillán, *Ricardo Flores Magón, el apostal de la revolución social mexicana* (Mexico, 1915), p. 75.

12. A useful chart listing the spasmodic editorial labors of the PLM from 1893–1918 is provided by Armando Bartra, *Regeneración, 1900–1918: La corriente más radical de la revolución de 1910 a través de su periódico de combate* (Mexico, 1972), pp. 67–71.

13. For the text of the manifesto of 1906 see Florencio Barrera Fuentes, *Historia de la revolución mexicana, la etapa pecursora* (Mexico, 1955), pp. 166–193.

14. Samuel Gompers, *Seventy Years of Life and Labour* (New York, 1925), 2: 303.

15. Flores Magón's political progress is demonstrated in the appendix in Juan Gómez-Quiñones, *Sembradores: Ricardo Flores Magón y El Partido Liberal Mexicano: A Eulogy and Critique* (Los Angeles, 1973).

16. John M. Hart, *Los Anarquistas Mexicanos, 1860–1900* (Mexico, 1974), p. 149. Blake A. Brophy, *Foundlings on the Frontier: Racial and Religious Conflict in Arizona Territory, 1904–1905* (Tucson, 1972), p. 17. Lorena M. Parlee, "The Impact of the United States Railroad Unions on Organized Labor and Government Policy in Mexico (1880–1911)," *Hispanic American Historical Review* (August, 1984), pp. 450, 453, 473. Richard U. Miller, "American Railroad Unions and the National Railways of Mexico. An Exercise in Nineteenth-Century Proletarian Manifest Destiny," *Labor History* (Spring 1974), pp. 239–260.

17. Readers were advised to go on strike, "to destroy the factory, block up the mine, devastate the farm." "To Swell the Ranks," *Reforma, Libertad, y Justicia* (June 15, 1908), National Archive, thereafter NA., RG 60, 90755. Just when Ricardo Flores Magón became an anarchist is difficult to determine. He may have been a "natural" anarchist long before his formal acceptance of anarchism. Hart indicates that he had become an anarchist by 1900, even before he fled Mexico. John M. Hart, *Revolutionary Mexico: The Coming and Process of the Mexican Revolution* (Berkeley, 1987), p. 91.

18. The definition of political repression used or implied throughout this study is that developed by Robert J. Goldstein as follows: Political repression consists of government action which grossly discriminates against persons or organizations viewed as presenting a fundamental challenge to existing power relationships or key governmental policies, because of their perceived political beliefs. Robert Justin Goldstein, *Political Repression in Modern America From 1870 to the Present* (Cambridge, Mass., 1978), p. xvi.

19. As Dirk Raat has emphasized repeatedly it is necessary to keep in mind the dangers of "precursorism" where one incident or individual automatically supplies the antecedents of another even more important event. Nevertheless, connections must be made. To

avoid making them when appropriate, and after careful consideration, leads to a sterile, ahistorical approach.
20. *Regeneración* (June, 1911).
21. Blaisdell recognized that Ricardo Flores Magón viewed himself in the broader context of worldwide revolution. Lowell L. Blaisdell, *The Desert Revolution: Baja California, 1911* (Madison, 1962), pp.
xii–xiii. One of the first to recognize Ricardo Flores Magón's political
contribution to the Mexican-American community in particular, was
Juan Gómez-Quiñones in his *Sembradores Ricardo Flores Magón y El
Partido Liberal Mexicano: A Eulogy and Critique* (Los Angeles, 1973).
See review by John M. Hart in *The Americas* (April 1975), pp. 535–
536. Parallels between Flores Magón and other revolutionaries have
been drawn by Gonzálo Aguirre Beltrán, ed., *Ricardo Flores Magón,
Antologia* (Mexico, 1970), p. x, and more extensively by Robert E. Ire-
land, "The Radical Community, Mexican and American Radicalism,
1900–1910," *Journal of Mexican American History* (Fall 1971), pp. 22–32.
22. For an approach that places the PLM and Ricardo Flores
Magón within the context of Mexican political exile activity in the
United States see W. Dirk Raat, *Revoltosos: Mexico's Rebels in the
United States, 1903–1923* (College Station, 1981).

2: Arizona, 1909

1. Joseph R. Conlin, *Big Bill Haywood and the Radical Union Movement* (Syracuse, 1969), pp. 12–15. The transformation of the region
is exemplified by Cananea, Sonora. From a small village of less than
100 in 1891 it grew to some 14,891 before 1910. A short rail connection tied the Cananea mine into the transborder economy. Salvador
Hernández, *Magonismo y Movimiento Obrero en Mexico: Cananea y Río
Blanco* (Mexico, 1977), p. 9.
2. The changing nature of the Southwest's economy, and its
growing dependency on large scale capitalization produced a number of "copper kings" tied to New York money markets. William C.
Greene represented the new type of entrepreneur in the region.
His operations involved mining and cattle and spanned the border.
C. L. Sonnichsen, *Colonel Greene and the Copper Skyrocket* (Tucson,
1974).
3. For a detailed view of a number of promoters see David M.
Pletcher, *Rails, Mines, and Progress: Seven American Promoters in
Mexico, 1867–1911* (Ithaca, 1958). Information on the financial careers
of a number of mining capitalists, and the extent of foreign capital
in the Mexican mining industry is documented in Marvin D. Bernstein, *The Mexican Mining Industry, 1890–1950: A Study of the Interaction of Politics, Economics, and Technology* (Albany, 1965), pp. 49–77.

4. Lawrence A. Cardoso, *Mexican Emigration to the United States 1897–1931: Socio-Economic Patterns* (Tucson, 1980), p. 29.

5. Leobardo F. Estrada, F. Chris García, Reynaldo Flores Macías, and Lionel Maldonado, "Chicanos in the United States: A History of Exploitation and Resistance," *Daedalus* (Spring 1981), p. 112.

6. Samuel Gompers, "United States—Mexico—Labor—Their Relations," *American Federationist* (August 1916), p. 633. Mexico's geographical proximity appealed to both capital and labor. While Gompers's international unionism appeared rather tame; on the other extreme, American IWW agitators in the Tampico oil fields horrified oil men and led to a newspaper campaign against the IWW in the Mexican and United States press. Marjorie Ruth Clark, *Organized Labor in Mexico* (Chapel Hill, 1934), p. 81. For the AFL approach, see Sinclair Snow, *The Pan-American Federation of Labor* (Durham, 1964).

7. Cletus E. Daniel, *Bitter Harvest: A History of California Farmworkers, 1870–1941* (Ithaca, 1981) pp. 77–78. Philip S. Foner, *History of the Labor Movement in the United States* (New York, 1964), 3: 276–277. For the situation in the border city of El Paso see Mario T. García, *Desert Immigrants: The Mexicans of El Paso, 1880–1920* (New Haven, 1981), pp. 85–109.

8. Ricardo Flores Magón to Roosevelt, September 12, 1906, NA., RG 59, 100/88–89. The letter represented one of the first policy statements concerning the relationship between the PLM and the United States. Charles Jacob Hanlen, "Ricardo Flores Magón: Biography of A Revolutionary" (M.A. thesis, University of San Diego, 1967), pp. 58–60.

9. James Joll, *The Anarchists* (New York, 1966) p. 176. After brief consideration the State Department decided no action was warranted. Ward Sloan Albro, "Ricardo Flores Magón and the Liberal Party: An Inquiry into the Origins of the Mexican Revolution of 1910" (Ph.D. diss., University of Arizona, 1967), pp. 83–84.

10. Sidney Fine, "Anarchism and the Assassination of McKinley," *American Historical Review* (July 1955), p. 780.

11. William Preston, Jr., *Aliens and Dissenters* (New York, 1966), p. 31.

12. Goldstein, *Political Repression in Modern America*, p. 68.

13. Fine, "Anarchism and the Assassination of McKinley," p. 793.

14. Goldstein, *Political Repression in Modern America*, pp. 68–69.

15. Manuel González Ramírez, *Fuentes para la historia de la Revolución Mexicana*, 4 vols. (Mexico, 1954–1957), 3: *La huelga de Cananea* provides a detailed account.

16. William Dirk Raat, "The Diplomacy of Suppression: Los Revoltosos, Mexico and the United States, 1906–1911," *Hispanic American Historical Review* (November 1976), p. 537. Varying opinions as

to the extent of PLM involvement are discussed in Rodney D. Anderson, *Outcasts in Their Own Land: Mexican Industrial Workers 1906–1911* (DeKalb, 1976), pp. 114–117.

17. Alan Knight, *The Mexican Revolution* (Cambridge, 1986), 1: 135–138. Barry Carr, *El movimiento obrero y la política en Mexico, 1910–1929* (Mexico, 1976), 1: 55–120.

18. Manuel González Ramírez, ed. *Epistolario y textos de Ricardo Flores Magón* (Mexico, 1964), pp. 172–173.

19. Thompson to Bacon, Sept. 5, 1906, NA., RG 59, 100/20.

20. James Brown Scott, "Memorandum in regard to the expulsion of certain Mexican citizens now held as prisoners at Nogales by Inspector Webb of Arizona" (Sept. 10, 1906), NA., RG 59, 100/30.

21. García, *Desert Immigrants*, pp. 176–177.

22. Raat, *Diplomacy*, p. 538.

23. The Mexican government circulated a picture of Flores Magón, and offered a 25,000 peso reward for his capture. González Ramírez, *Epistolario*, p. 92.

24. John M. Hart, *Revolutionary Mexico. The Coming and Process of the Mexican Revolution.* (Berkeley, 1987), pp. 94–95. Paul J. Vanderwood provided a chilling description of the economic situation in *Disorder and Progress: Bandits, Police, and Mexican Development* (Lincoln, 1981), pp. 141–147. Linda B. Hall, *Alvaro Obregón: Power and Revolution in Mexico, 1911–1920* (College Station, 1981), p. 16.

25. Thomas Furlong, *Fifty Years a Detective* (St. Louis, 1912), pp. 142–143. Three members of the Los Angeles Police force involved in the arrest, detectives Felipe Talamantes, Louis Rico, and Thomas Rico apparently acted under the direction of Ambassador Creel and Antonio Lozano, the Mexican consul in Los Angeles. Subsequently, the three detectives faced a police commission investigation on the issue as well as other charges. All three were acquitted. Edward J. Escobar, "Mexican Revolutionaries and the Los Angeles Police: Harassment of the Partido Liberal Mexicano, 1907–1910," *Azátlan* (Spring 1986), pp. 27–29.

26. Lyle C. Brown, "The Mexican Liberals and Their Struggle Against the Díaz Dictatorship: 1900–1906," *Antologia Mexico City College* (Mexico, 1956), p. 354. The extradition treaty of 1899 excluded political acts, therefore a criminal charge had to be made. James Morton Callahan, *American Foreign Policy in Mexican Relations* (New York, 1967), p. 442. An arrest warrant dated August 29, 1907, six days after the actual arrest set forth the charges. It would not be officially executed until September 16, 1907. *Warrant to Apprehend and Affidavid of Complaint* (August 29, 1907), Federal Records Center, Los Angeles, hereafter (FRC-LA), Record Group RG 21, case 573.

27. Jesús Flores Magón to Roosevelt, NA., RG 59, number 178, 1741/94, 60.

28. Ward Sloan Albro, III, "Ricardo Flores Magón and the Liberal

Party: An Inquiry Into the Origins of the Mexican Revolution of 1910" (Ph.D. diss., University of Arizona, 1967), p. 139. Years later Lawler fondly recalled "Ricky" Creel as an old friend; unfortunately, he only vaguely remembered the Flores Magón case, observing that Enrique was the leader who was defended by Job Harriman, a likeable individual but an "extreme socialist." Oscar Lawler, "Oral History Interview," *Oral History Project*, UCLA (1962), pp. 28, 60.

29. *Indictment, Grand Jury of the United States of America, Second Judicial District of the Territory of Arizona* (December 28, 1907), FRC-LA, RG 21, case 669.

30. Judge Fletcher M. Doan, on the motion of the U.S. Attorney, *Fixed Bail. Order for Bench Warrant and Fixing Bail* (December 30, 1970), FRC-LA, RG 21, case 660.

31. "Manifesto to the American People," *Mother Earth* (February 1908), pp. 546–554.

32. Ellen Howell Myers, "The Mexican Liberal Party, 1903–1910" (Ph.D. diss., University of Virginia, 1971), p. 231.

33. Eugene V. Debs, "This Plot Must Be Foiled," *Appeal To Reason* (October 10, 1908), p. 2.

34. The Los Angeles Labor Council compared the Mexican government's attempt to secure extradition to King George III's desire to apprehend George Washington, "Los Angeles Labor Council to Organized Labor," *Miner's Magazine* (March 26, 1908), p. 12.

35. *President Gompers Presents the Case of the Imprisoned Mexican Patriots to President Roosevelt* (Chicago, 1909).

36. Samuel Gompers, *Seventy Years of Life and Labour* (New York, 1925), 2: 309. Technically the House of Representatives adopted a resolution (April 21, 1910) asking the attorney general for information only, and he replied as requested. The results were minimal serving only to make the attorney general aware of the political sensitivity of the Flores Magón case, and the Left's ability to muster some support in Congress. *Resolution: Requesting Information of the Attorney General Concerning the Imprisonment of Certain Persons at Florence, Arizona*, NA., RG 60, 90755.

37. Dale Fetherling, *Mother Jones, the Miners' Angel: A Portrait* (Carbondale, 1974), p. 81. Edward M. Steel, ed. *The Speeches and Writings of Mother Jones* (Pittsburgh, 1988), pp. 28–29.

38. Mary Harris Jones, *Autobiography of Mother Jones* (New York, 1969), pp. 140–142.

39. United States House of Representatives, *Hearing on the House Joint Resolution 210 Providing for a Joint Committee to Investigate Alleged Persecutions of Mexican Citizens by the Government of Mexico* (Washington, D.C., 1910), pp. 90–91. Murray and Turner wrote letters to officials stressing the Mexican government's power in the United States. Turner claimed that law in the border states had been "Mex-

icanized" as far as Mexican citizens were concerned. *Congressional Record—House* (April 21, 1910), 45: pt. 5, p. 5137. Murray had spent some time in jail falsely charged with conspiracy to assassinate President Taft when he met with President Díaz on El Paso's International Bridge. Snow, *The Pan-American Federation*, p. 7.

40. Attorney General to Secretary of Commerce and Labor (June 19, 1911), NA., RG 60, 90755.

41. Manuel Sarabia's marriage took Flores Magón by surprise. He had viewed Miss Trowbridge's help as totally disinterested. González Ramírez, *Epistolario*, p. 192.

42. *Appeal to Reason* (March 13, 1909), pp. 1–2.

43. Oscar Lawler to the Attorney General (July 6, 1908), NA., RG 60, 90755. W. Dirk Raat, *Revoltosos: Mexico's Rebels in the United States, 1903–1923* (College Station, 1981), p. 161.

44. Oscar Lawler to Attorney General (April 20, 1909), NA., RG 60, 90755.

45. W. H. H. Llewellyn to Attorney General (March 31, 1909), NA., RG 60, 90755.

46. *Sensational Cause. The Mexican Revolutionists Before the United States Justice* (May 1909), NA., RG 60, 90755.

47. *Patriotic Liberal Junta of Ladies and Young Ladies of Juárez and Lerdo in Rotan, Texas* (January 21, 1909), NA., RG 60, 90755.

48. Petition from Local No. 215, Women's International Union Label League to Attorney General Wickersham, NA., RG 60, 90755.

49. González Ramírez, *Epistolario*, p. 223.

50. Harriman and Holston were law-firm partners. In 1900 the national convention of the Social Democratic Party nominated Eugene V. Debs for president and Harriman as vice-president; the ticket drew 97,000 votes. Harriman, along with Morris Hillquit and other Social Labor Party insurgents, joined with Debs to form the Socialist Party of America in 1901. He authored *The Class Struggle in Idaho in 1904*. Harriman had a reputation as a pragmatic socialist willing to work with all elements of the Left; as a result he put together a coalition that almost elected him mayor of Los Angeles. Knox Mellon, Jr., "Job Harriman: The Early and Middle Years, 1861–1921" (Ph.D. diss., Claremont Graduate School, 1972), pp. 42, 172–186. Melvyn Dubofsky, *We Shall Be All: A History of the Industrial Workers of the World* (New York, 1969), pp. 63, 69.

51. In early 1908 Harriman unsuccessfully petitioned the U.S. Supreme Court for bail reduction and again asking for a writ of habeas corpus. Appellant Case No. 21153, NA., RG 267. Application of R. Flores Magón et al., for a Writ of Habeas Corpus, NA. RG 267. "R. Flores Magón, et al., Appellant v. United States (January 4, 1909)," *Supreme Court Reporter* (December 1908–July 1909), vol. 29, 690.

52. Manuel Sarabia already had experienced an illegal extradition in Douglas, Arizona after being arrested by American officials, then taken from jail at night and delivered to Mexican authorities. The subsequent uproar embarrassed both governments to the point that Sarabia was returned to American jurisdiction. At Harriman's request, U.S. Senator Perkins conveyed the fear of a repetition if the men were sent to Arizona for trial. Ethel Dolsen, "Mexican Revolutionists in the United States," *Miner's Magazine* (June 11, 1908), p. 9. Sarabia recounted the incident in "How I Was Kidnaped: Story of My Escape From the Rurales and Hermosillo Penitentiary," in Elizabeth D. Trowbridge, *Political Prisoners Held in the United States: Refugees Imprisoned at the Request of a Foreign Government,* John Murray Collection, Bancroft Library, University of California, Berkeley. Sarabia was indicted for violation of the neutrality laws in January 1908 and subsequently ordered removed to Tombstone, Arizona. In May he was extradited and secretly transferred without his lawyer's knowledge giving rise to fears of another kidnapping. Finally released on bond he fled to Europe. *United States of America, Plaintiff vs. Manuel Sarabia,* FRC-LA, RG 21, case 26.

53. Alexander insisted that they intended to assassinate high officials, blow up railroads, and commit other such crimes. Albro, *Ricardo Flores Magón,* p. 146. Alexander asked that Lawler be appointed a special assistant in order to take part in the prosecution; however, before the trial began he resigned his post to assume the position of the Assistant Attorney General assigned to the Interior Department. Attorney General to J. L. B. Alexander (March 31, 1909), NA., RG 60, 90755. Luther T. Ellsworth, U.S. Consul at Ciudad Porfirio Díaz just across the border from Eagle Pass, Texas, claimed that the American Socialist Party financed the *Magonistas* in their attempt to overthrow Díaz. Dorothy Pierson Kerig, *Luther T. Ellsworth, U.S. Consul on the Border During the Mexican Revolution* (El Paso, 1975), p. 21.

54. *Commisioner's Transcript* (November 1907), FRC-LA, RG 21, case 582. James D. Cockcroft, *Intellectual Precursors of the Mexican Revolution, 1900–1913*(Austin, 1968), p. 137. Richard H. Frost, *The Mooney Case* (Stanford, 1968), p. 47.

55. *Appeal to Reason* (March 27, 1909) p. 1.

56. Dirk Raat, *Revoltosos: Mexico's Rebels in the United States, 1903–1923* (College Station, 1981), pp. 44–45. Harrison George, *The IWW Trial: Story of the Greatest Trial in Labor History by One of the Defendants* (New York, 1969), p. 12.

57. *Motion for a New Trial* (May 17, 1909), FRC-LA, RG 21, case 693.

58. *Tucson Citizen* (May 15, 1909), p. 1.

59. *Motion for a New Trial* (May 17, 1909), FRC-LA, RG 21, case 693.

60. J. L. B. Alexander to Attorney General (April 12, 1909). V. Salado Alvarez, First Secretary of the Mexican Embassy, to Attorney General (May 8, 1909), NA., RG 60, 90755.

61. The convicted conspirators were sent to Yuma, then in September they were transferred to the new penitentiary at Florence, Arizona. At the suggestion of the Mexican Consul in Phoenix, the Mexican government offered Alexander $500 in appreciation. He declined the offer, but later accepted a $475 diamond ring delicately presented by a grateful Mexican government. González Ramírez, *Epistolario,* p. 161.

62. Ethel Duffy Turner, *Ricardo Flores Magón y el Partido Liberal Mexicano* (Morelia, 1960), p. 193. John Kenneth Turner wrote a long article to the *Appeal* describing the release. *Appeal to Reason* (August 13, 1910), p. 1.

63. Ibid., pp. 193–194.

64. In a letter to Enrique, Ricardo wrote that "the United States is truly a country of pigs. Look at the socialists: they cowardly break up their free speech campaign. Look at the resplendent American Federation of Labor with its million and a half members which cannot prevent injunctions." Abad de Santillán, *Ricardo Flores Magón,* pp. 47–55. Ricardo expressed his irritation with the stereotype in a letter to María Flores Magón. González Ramírez, *Epistolario,* p. 169.

65. In a like manner William C. Owen flatly stated that the question "is not Mexican but international." William C. Owen, "Viva Mexico," *Mother Earth* (April 1911), p. 46.

66. *Mother Earth* (December 1909), pp. 321–323. In the same fashion Debs hammered at the "Russianization" and "Mexicanization" of American judiciary that made it possible to persecute the PLM and the three men in Florence. Debs accused Attorney General Wickersham of defending his interest in the Mexican Central Railway in conjunction with Wall Street interests. Eugene V. Debs, "You Will Reap the Whirlwind," *Appeal to Reason* (November 6, 1909), p. 4.

67. Eugene V. Debs, *Writings and Speeches of Eugene V. Debs* (New York, 1948), p. 339.

68. González Ramírez, *Epistolario,* p. 206.

3: LOS ANGELES, 1912

1. David G. LaFrance, *The Mexican Revolution in Puebla, 1908–1913* (Wilmington, Del., 1989), pp. 5–8.

2. Ricardo Flores Magón, "The Appeal of Mexico to American Labor," *Mother Earth* (April 1911), pp. 47–48; Flores Magón to Goldman, March 13, 1911, *Mother Earth* (April 1911), pp. 48–49.

3. Ivie E. Cadenhead, Jr. "The American Socialists and the Mexican Revolution of 1910," *Southwestern Social Science Quarterly* (September 1962), p. 109.

4. Agustín Cúe Cánovas, *Ricardo Flores Magón, la Baja California y los Estados Unidos* (Mexico, 1957), p. 106. Participation of foreigners in PLM activities, among other factors, contributed to the alienation of Flores Magón followers including Gutiérrez de Lara, Antonio I. Villarreal, and José María Leyva who joined with Madero. Stanley R. Ross, *Francisco I. Madero: Apostle of Mexican Democracy* (New York, 1955), p. 145.

5. Lowell L. Blaisdell, *The Desert Revolution, Baja California, 1911* (Madison, 1962), pp. 154–155. The *Herald* carried a photograph of Ferris under the caption, "First President of the Republic of Lower California," *Los Angeles Herald* (June 3, 1911), p. 12. W. Dirk Raat, *Revoltosos: Mexico's Rebels in the United States, 1903–1923* (College Station, 1981), p. 57.

6. Edward M. Steel, ed. *The Speeches and Writings of Mother Jones* (Pittsburgh, 1988), p. 309 and *The Correspondence of Mother Jones,* (Pittsburgh, 1985), pp. 97–100.

7. *Appeal to Reason* (May 27, 1911), p. 4.

8. Ibid. (February 4, 1911), p. 4. In May the *Appeal* declared the Mexican revolution over, and took full credit for a "remarkable historical event that was practically inaugurated by the *Appeal to Reason.*" Ibid. (May 27, 1911), p. 4.

9. *New York Call* (March 7, 1911), p. 1. The *Call* headlined "Madero Traitor to the People of Mexico."

10. Ibid. (April 12, 1911), p. 3. The paper claimed that Flores Magón operated from the perfect security of his Los Angeles office, and used his newspaper to denounce socialists in spite of the fact that many socialists faced federal rifles in Baja California.

11. *Regeneración* (April 15, 1911).

12. Quoted in *Mother Earth* (July 1911), p. 132.

13. "An Open Letter from Juan Sarabia to Ricardo Flores Magón," *New York Call* (August 2, 1911), p. 6.

14. Ibid.

15. Abad de Santillán, *Ricardo Flores Magón,* pp. 87, 90–94.

16. Ricardo Flores Magón, *Vida y Obra* (Mexico, D.F., 1923–1925), 2: 31–35.

17. Abad de Santillán, *Ricardo Flores Magón,* pp. 87, 90–94.

18. Reichert links Berkman's act with the medieval theory of tyranicide. Violence is justified as the last resort. William O. Reichert, *Partisans of Freedom: A Study in American Anarchism* (Bowling Green, Ohio, 1976), p. 410.

19. Ibid. Ambivalence on the subject of violence is evident in Emma Goldman's letter to Ben Reitman on the subject, "violence is inevitable . . . because it is thrust upon the individual and the masses by conditions. Now, whether I would or would not use violence, I never have or would condemn the individual in his struggle

with society if he uses violence." Quoted in Candace Falk, *Love, Anarchy and Emma Goldman* (New York, 1984), p. 229. An equally shaded approach to the notion of violence appears in "The Psychology of Political Violence," in Emma Goldman's *Anarchism and Other Essays* (New York, 1911), pp. 85–114. Kropotkin's similar attitude is captured in Richard Polenberg, *Fighting Faiths: The Abrams Case, the Supreme Court and Free Speech* (New York, 1987), pp. 20–21.

20. Letter of July 21, 1911 published in *Mother Earth* (August 1911), pp. 161–162. Both Mother Jones and Job Harriman were alienated in the aftermath of the Baja failure. W. Dirk Raat, *Revoltosos: Mexico's Rebels in the United States, 1903–1923* (College Station, 1981), p. 59. While Mother Jones worked against the PLM Harriman continued to help Flores Magón, although perhaps with less fervor.

21. Owen accused the socialists of avoiding the true revolutionary situation in Mexico to concentrate on Harriman's race for Los Angeles mayor. Rather unfairly he observed that the Socialist party was not a friend but an enemy, "I regret it deeply, but facts are facts." William C. Owen, "Mexico and Socialism," *Mother Earth* (September 1911), pp. 199–202.

22. De la Barra to Minister of Foreign Affairs (October 28, 1910) in Isidro and Josefina E. Fabela, eds., *Documentos históricos de la Revolución Mexicana* (Mexico, 1966), pp. 10, 101–103.

23. *Mother Earth* (June 1911), pp. 98–99. In the same vein, see William C. Owen, "Mexico's Hour of Need," ibid., 105–107. Other members of the Mexican Revolutionary Conference were Harry Kelly, Leonard D. Abbott, and Milo Harvey Woolman. Ibid. (September 1911), pp. 195–197.

24. *Regeneración* (June 24, 1911). Madero supporters worked to disband armed PLM groups and successfully "mustered out" PLM soldiers at Mexicali, but failed to make much headway at Tijuana. Even this limited success of the anti-Flores Magón forces indicated the ideological weakness that plagued the PLM. William H. Beezley, *Insurgent Governor: Abraham González and the Mexican Revolution in Chihuahua* (Lincoln, 1973), p. 91.

25. Blaisdell, *The Desert Revolution*, p. 170.

26. Attorney General to A. I. McCormick, U.S. Attorney, Los Angeles (May 27, 1911), NA., RG 60, 90755.

27. Indictment, *Grand Jury of the United States of America, U.S. District Court, Southern District, Southern Division* (July 8, 1911), FRC-LA, RG 21, case 374 and 375. The Texas indictment (October 12, 1908) remained outstanding, and still served as a backup. Attorney General to W. H. H. Llewellyn, Special Assistant to the Attorney General, Las Cruces, New Mexico (June 13, 1911), NA., RG 60, 90755.

28. Demurrer (July 31, 1911), FRC-LA, RG 21, case 374–375.

29. *Los Angeles Times* (June 2, 1912), pt. 5, 23.

30. A. I. McCormick to Attorney General (April 8, 1912), NA., RG 60, 90755.

31. Fowler, Assistant to the Attorney General to A. I. McCormick (April 18, 1912), NA., RG 60, 90755.

32. *Mother Earth* (September, 1911), pp. 223–224. Neno Vasco (Gregório Nazianzeno Moreira de Queiros Vasconcelos) lived in Brazil from 1901 to 1910 where he was closely associated with Brazilian anarchist Edgard Leuenroth, editor of *Lantera*. John W. F. Dulles, *Anarchists and Communists in Brazil, 1900–1935* (Austin, 1973), pp. 9, 15. For some interesting fragments of information on Brazilian anarchist see Paul Avrich, *Anarchist Portraits* (Princeton, 1988), pp. 255–259.

33. "Report of the Work of the Chicago Mexican Liberal Defense League," *Mother Earth* (April, 1912), pp. 60–62.

34. The collection is in NA., RG 60, 90755.

35. The best account of the struggle over the open shop and the part played by the *Los Angeles Times* is provided by Grace H. Stimpson, *The Rise of the Labor Movement in Los Angeles* (Berkeley, 1955).

36. Lozano to Minister of Foreign Affairs (October 10, 1910); Isidro Fabela and Josefina E. Fabela, eds., *Documentos históricos de la Revolución Mexicana*, 10: 100.

37. Patrick Renshaw, *The Wobblies: The Story of Syndicalism in the United States* (New York, 1968), p. 90.

38. Rev. Charles Edmund Locke of the First Methodist Church, taking the *Times* bombing as his topic, mirrored public opinion when he declared that the country had been: "Too tardy and lenient in our efforts to suppress dangerous public utterances in this land of free speech. The vicious acts of these murderers is the logical sequence . . . of loud-mouthed anarchists . . . Our watchword must be the extermination of anarchists and anarchy. They are a greater danger than the bubonic plague, and every suspect should be arrested and quarantined. Eternal vigilance is the price of liberty." *Los Angeles Times* (October 10, 1910), p. 12.

39. Emma Goldman, *Living My Life* (New York, 1970), p. 478.

40. Hyman Weintraub, "The IWW in California, 1905–1931" (M.A. thesis, University of California, Los Angeles, 1947), p. 40. For a vivid description see Philip S. Foner, *The Industrial Workers of the World, 1905–1917* (New York, 1965), pp. 194–205.

41. Motion of Substitute Attorney, FRC-LA, RG 21, case 374 and 375.

42. *Los Angeles Times* (June 5, 1912), pt. 1, p. 7.

43. Bill Haywood subsequently recalled that most members of the Brawley and Imperial IWW locals joined with the Mexican revolutionists. Many continued to support Flores Magón. William D.

Haywood, *Bill Haywood's Book: The Autobiography of William D. Haywood* (New York, 1929), p. 276.

44. Senate Documents, 66th Congress, 2 Session 1919–1920, *Investigation of Mexican Affairs* (Washington, 1920), 1: 2518.

45. Blaisdell, *The Desert Revolution*, p. 190. Federal Attorneys apparently felt themselves under pressure to secure convictions in political cases and resorted to doubtful witnesses. In another incident involving Harry Chandler, son-in-law of Harrison Gray Otis, the district attorney, prodded by the democratic administration of Woodrow Wilson, introduced questionable witnesses in an attempt to sustain a charge of neutrality law violation. Two of the witnesses indicated a willingness to disappear in return for $2,000. The judge directed the jury to return a verdict of acquittal. Lowell L. Blaisdell, "Harry Chandler and Mexican Border Intrigue, 1914–1917," *Pacific Historical Review* (November 1966), p. 391.

46. Langham observed that Willedd Andrew's inexperience hindered the defense. He failed to exploit Martin's admission, and as a result it had little impact on the jury. Thomas C. Langham, *Border Trials: Ricardo Flores Magón and the Mexican Liberals* (El Paso, 1981), pp. 45–46.

47. *Los Angeles Times* (June 5, 1912), pt. 1, 7. For Limón, arbitrary arrest was becoming a pattern. The LAPD had arrested him on October 10, 1909 for protesting the seizure of Lázaro Gutiérrez de Lara for making an anti-Díaz speech. Edward J. Escobar, "Mexican Revolutionaries and the Los Angeles Police: Harassment of the Partido Liberal Mexicano, 1907–1910," *Azātln* (Spring 1986), p. 18.

48. Langham. p. 46.

49. *Prosecution Instructions to the Jury* (June 21 Ä?Ü, 1912), FRC-LA, RG 21, case 374 and 375.

50. *Defendant's Jury Instruction* (June 21, 1912), FRC-LA, RG 21, case 374 and 375.

51. *Instructions of the Court* (June 21, 1912), FRC-LA, RG 21, case 374 and 375.

52. *Los Angeles Times* (June 23, 1912), pt. 2, 1.

53. *Sentence of Defendants Ricardo Flores Magón, Librado Rivera and Anselmo L. Figueroa* (June 25, 1912), FRC-LA, RG 21, case 374–375.

54. *Los Angeles Examiner* (June 25, 1912).

55. Ibid. (July 5, 1912).

56. *Mother Earth* (May 1913), pp. 72–73.

57. Blaisdell, *The Desert Revolution*, p. 12.

4: "LET THE COURT SPEAK! HISTORY WATCHES!"
LOS ANGELES, 1916

1. "Bernard Shaw Shies at American Bastiles," *Wilshire's Magazine* (May 1913), p. 5. Gaylord Wilshire had earlier recommended

that those interested in understanding the Mexican revolution should read *Regeneración*. "The Mexican Revolution," *Wilshire's Magazine* (August 1912), p. 4. Wilshire was viewed as an eccentric. Los Angeles' Wilshire Boulevard bears his name. For details on Wilshire and other "millionaire" socialists see David A. Shannon, *The Socialist Party of America: A History* (New York, 1955), p. 58.

2. "The Mexican Comrades at McNeil," *Why?* (September, 1913), pp. 5–6.

3. Preston, p. 57 and Goldstein, pp. 90–91.

4. John M. Hart, *Anarchism and the Mexican Working Class, 1860–1931* (Austin, 1978), pp. 111–114.

5. *Regeneración* (February 15, 1913). The *casa* did not become a success. After inspection by the authorities, the building was declared unsafe because it was not fireproof, thus forcing *Regeneración* to move to a new location on Boston Street. The Building remained in the hands of Enrique Flores Magón's father-in-law for another year. Ethel Duffy Turner, *Ricardo Flores Magón y el Partido Liberal Mexicano* (Morelia, 1960), p. 282.

6. *Los Angeles Times* (February 9, 1913), 2: 1, 9.

7. *Regeneración* (January 24, 1914).

8. *Regeneración* (February 7, 1914).

9. Ethel Duffy Turner, *Ricardo Flores Magón*, p. 282.

10. *Regeneración* (January 31, 1914).

11. Ibid.

12. *Regeneración* (February 21, 1914).

13. Socialists developed their own explantation of Mexican affairs. The National Executive Committee claimed that Wall Street financed Villa and the government used border raids as a pretext for preparing for a Mexican war. While ambivalent about Wilson, Carranza received the backing of most socialists. Diana K. Christopulos, "American Radicals and the Mexican Revolution, 1900–1925" (Ph.D. diss., State University of New York at Binghamton, 1980), pp. 247–257.

14. Paul Avrich, *An American Anarchist: The Life of Voltairine de Cleyre* (Princeton, 1978), pp. 229–231.

15. Voltairine de Cleyre, "The Mexican Revolution," *Mother Earth* (December 1911 continued in January and February 1912), pp. 301–306, 335–341, 374–380.

16. Sinclair Snow, *The Pan-American Federation of Labor* (Durham, 1964), p. 15, John M. Hart, *Revolutionary Mexico: the Coming and Process of the Mexican Revolution* (Berkeley, 1987), p. 308. Harvey A. Levinstein, *Labor Organizations in the United States and Mexico* (Westport, 1971), p. 22.

17. After Carranza assumed power Gompers and Luis Morones of the Regional Confederation of Mexican Workers (CROM) worked

out the basic structure and objectives of the Pan American Federation of Labor—essentially a Latin American version of the AFL, Wilson viewed the PAFL as an AFL contribution to the war effort and underwrote its expenses. Ronald Radosh, *American Labor and United States Foreign Policy* (New York, 1969), p. 352.

18. In an article titled "Anti-Jingoes Win an Epoch-Making Victory; Why Wilson Turns Back from Mexican War," John Kenneth Turner gave credit for heading off American intervention to the Socialists of America, organized labor, advocates for peace, especially the American Union Against Militarism, the forebearance of Carranza and the armed strength of the Mexican government. The PLM received no credit. *Appeal to Reason* (July 22, 1916), p. 1. The *International Socialist Review* characterized Carranza's reforms as a "real" revolution. *International Socialist Review* (August, 1916), p. 87.

19. Alfonso López Aparicio, *El movimiento obrero en México: antecedents, desarrollo y tendencias* (Mexico, 1952), p. 158.

20. "Mexican Strikers May Get Death Penalty," *Mother Earth* (September 1916), pp. 612–615.

21. "The Organizing Junta of the Mexican Liberal Party to the Workers of the United States, November 7, 1914," *Mother Earth* (April, 1915), pp. 85–88.

22. Ibid.

23. In Mexico City the Casa del Obrero Mundial rejected Magonista tactics and one writer described the Los Angeles group as renegades thousands of miles away who are exaggerating events in Mexico. John M. Hart, *Anarchism and the Mexican Working Class, 1860–1931* (Austin, 1978), p. 129.

24. See the analysis of the Plan of Ayala in John Womack, Jr., *Zapata and the Mexican Revolution* (New York, 1969), pp. 393–404.

25. Armando Bartra, "La Otra Revolución Mexicana," *Siempre* (Diciembre 20, 1972), suplemento, p. 4. Lincoln Steffens, noted editor and muckraker, analyzed the PLM's failure as a result of "educated, fanatical revolutionary leaders "the Magoons" [sic] with a theory and plan" who ignored the fact that the Mexican revolution depended more on a reaction to oppression than on theories. Lincoln Steffens, *The Autobiography of Lincoln Steffens* (New York, 1931), p. 720. Steffens traveled with Carranza in 1915 and campaigned for his recognition by the United States. Christopulos, p. 258.

26. William C. Owen, "The Death of Ricardo Flores Magón," reprinted from *Freedom* (December 1922) in David Poole, ed. *Land and Liberty: Anarchist Influences in the Mexican Revolution—Ricardo Flores Magón* (Sanday, Orkney, 1977), pp. 115–119.

27. For an analysis of the plan's text see Juan Gómez Q, "Plan de San Diego Reviewed," *Aztlán* (Spring 1970), pp. 124–132. The plan has also been linked to followers of deposed, but still plotting,

ex-president Huerta. Michael C. Meyer, *Huerta: A Political Portrait* (Lincoln, 1972), p. 215. A convincing analysis separates the activities stimulated by the plan into stages, and suggests that Carranza skillfully used it to pressure the United States government to recognize his regime. Charles H. Harris III and Louis R. Sadler, "The Plan of San Diego and the Mexican-United States War Crisis of 1916: A Reexamination," *Hispanic American Historical Review* (August 1978), pp. 341–408, and by the same authors, *The Border and the Revolution* (Las Cruces, 1988), pp. 71–98.

28. Charles C. Cumberland, "Border Raids in the Lower Rio Grande Valley—1915," *Southwestern Historical Quarterly* (January 1954), pp. 291, 295. At least twenty-seven raids under its banner resulted in the social and economic disruption of four Texas counties, some thirty-three deaths, and twenty-four wounded. Luis de la Rosa, variously described as a Laredo butcher and a deputy sheriff, and Aniceto Pizaña, a small landholder, provided field leadership. James A. Sandos, "The Plan of San Diego: War and Diplomacy on the Texas Border, 1915–1916," *Arizona and the West* (Spring 1972), p. 23.

29. Harris and Sadler, *The Border and the Revolution*, p. 82.

30. Walter M. Cookson, Inspector Post Office Department to Inspector in Charge, San Francisco, California (n.d. 1915–early 1916), NA., RG 60, 90755.

31. Thirteen were of Mexican extraction and one, Charles Cline, was an IWW member. The group left Carrizo Springs, Texas, with the intention of entering Mexico; however, an overly zealous official, Dimmit County Sheriff Eugene Buck, and his deputy, Candelario Ortiz, followed them and shot one of the group before being seized by the men. Deputy Ortiz, in a rash attempt to escape, grappled with his guard and was killed. Sheriff Buck was exchanged in return for a safe conduct pledge which would be broken. Of the group the prosecution singled out Jesús M. Rangel, Eugenio Alzalde, José Abraham Cisneros, and Charles Cline as responsible for the deputy's death and asked for a capital penalty. "The Rangel-Cline Case," *Mother Earth* (June 1914), pp. 111–115. Elizabeth Gurley Flynn recalled and described the incident years later and quoted Texas Governor "Ma" Ferguson's comments in 1926 when she pardoned those involved that it "was no crime to overthrow the Mexican government any more than it was for those who defended the Alamo in 1836." Elizabeth Gurley Flynn, *I Speak My Own Piece: Autobiography of the Rebel Girl* (New York, 1955), p. 168.

32. Titled "Tierra y Libertad: Himno Revolucionario" with the following chorus:

> Proletarios: al grito de guerra
> por ideales luchado con valor,

y expropiad, attrevida, la tierra
que detenta nuestro explotador.
Regeneración (February 14, 1914).

33. *Los Angeles Times* (September 20, 1915), pt. 2, 1.
34. *Regeneración* (November 13, 1915).
35. *Indictment, Grand Jury of the United States of America, Southern Division of the Southern District of California* (February 18, 1916), FRC-LA, RG 21, case 1071.
36. Section 211 was one of a number of statutes enacted in 1873 under pressure from Anthony Comstock and his Society for the Suppression of Vice, supposedly to ensure sexual purity and guard women against harmful contraceptive devices and practices. The role of the so-called Comstock law in the struggle for birth control is portrayed in David M. Kennedy, *Birth Control in America* (New Haven, 1970). Section 211 thus prohibited any article or drug intended to prevent conception and induce abortion or for any "immoral" purpose. *The Federal Penal Code in Force, January 1, 1910* (Boston, 1910), p. 180. "An Act to Amend Section 211 Federal Penal Code of 1910," *U.S. Statutes at Large, 61st Congress (1900–1911)*, 36, pt. 1, p. 1339.
37. *Indictment* (February 18, 1916).
38. *Los Angeles Times* (February 19, 1916), pt. 2, 1. Owen remained a fugitive, but managed to continue sending articles for the English section until eventually he lost contact with the Los Angeles group. The *Examiner's* account reported that a "beautiful young girl, recognized as having taken part in a previous PLM disturbance, leaped at the arresting officers like a 'tigress'"; presumably they referred to Lucille, *Los Angeles Examiner* (February 19, 1916), pt. 2, 1.
39. *Los Angeles Times* (February 20, 1916), pt. 2, 11. *Los Angeles Examiner* (February 22, 1916), pt. 2, 1.
40. Ibid. (February 25, 1916), p. 1, 5.
41. James H. Ryckman, a one-time partner of Job Harriman, had a well-established and respected reputation for his defense of the poor, pacifists, and IWW defendants. A socialist in the same mold as Harriman, he wrote and lectured widely. From 1919 to 1920 he wrote the "Truth About Russia" section in the *New Justice*. In 1924 he worked for the election of LaFollete. He was often referred to as Judge Ryckman out of respect. Rockwell D. Hunt, ed., *California and Californians* (Los Angeles, 1930), 3: 239–240. Ernest E. Kirk, known as "pink whiskers" because of his reddish whiskers, associated with Flores Magón in 1911 probably through Emma Goldman. Kirk, Ben Reitman, and Goldman visited Jack London during one of Emma's tours of the West. *Mother Earth* (June 1910), p. 126. By his own account, Kirk dropped socialism in 1916, apparently after the Flores Magón's trial, becoming quite conservative. He became the ranking

National Guard officer in Los Angeles during World War I and at the time of his death served as Burbank city attorney. Leland G. Stanford, *Footprints of Justice in San Diego and Profiles of Senior Members of the Bench and Bar* (San Diego, 1960), p. 30; and the *Los Angeles Times* (July 30, 1921), pt. 2, 1.

42. *Mother Earth* (March 1916), pp. 419–420.

43. "A Letter from María Flores Magón," *Blast* (February 26, 1961), p. 6.

44. "Muzzling Discontent," *Blast* (February 26, 1916), p. 5; and "Come Workers, Let Us Take Counsel Together," *Blast* (July 15, 1916), p. 2.

45. "Brave Voices from Prison," *Blast* (March 15, 1916), p. 4.

46. "America and Mexico," *Mother Earth* (April 1916), pp. 488–490. William Charles Owen (1854–1929) spent thirty-two years in the United States. His father served as the director of a military hospital in British India. Well educated, proficient in a number of languages, Owen spent his last years in England living in poverty, a dedicated anarchist to the end. He proved an insightful critic of the labor party. For interesting details see William O. Reichert, *Partisans of Freedom: A Study in American Anarchism* (Bowling Green, Ohio, 1976), pp. 512–519.

47. Richard H. Frost, *The Mooney Case* (Stanford, 1968), p. 37. The IWDL had originally been organized in San Francisco in 1912 to aid radicals. It represented a rare nonsectarian effort by all radical groups except the Socialist Labor Party.

48. Edgecomb Pinchon, "Think of the Magóns," *Blast* (June 1, 1916), p. 2.

49. *Demurrer* (ca. March 13, 1916), FRC-LA, RG 21, case 1071.

50. *Los Angeles Times* (March 14, 1916), pt. 1, 7.

51. Ibid., and *Court Ruling on Demurrer* (March 13, 1916), *Motion to Quash Indictment* (May 31, 1916), FRC-LA, RG 21, case 1071.

52. *Los Angeles Times* (May 9, 1916), pt. 2, 8 and *Report of E. H. Garrett, M.D., Surgeon in Charge of U.S. Prisoners* (May 8, 1916), FRC-LA, RG 21, case 1071.

53. *Los Angeles Times* (May 10, 1916), pt. 2, 1.

54. *Mailing List of Regeneración* (U.S. Exhibits 15, 16, 17 and 18), FRC-LA, RG 21, case 1071.

55. *Motion for New Trial* (ca. June 23, 1916), FRC-LA, RG 21, case 1071.

56. "The Magón Case," *Blast* (April 15, 1916), p. 4.

57. "The Bloodhounds," ibid., p. 2.

58. "A Last Call to Radicals," *Blast* (September 15, 1916), p. 2.

59. *Los Angeles Times* (June 2, 1916), pt. 2, 2.

60. *Trial Record* (May 31, 1916), FRC-LA, RG 21, case 1071.

61. *Blast* (February 26, 1916), p. 6.

62. *Statement of Defendant Enrique Flores Magón* (June 3, 1916). FRC-LA, RG 21, case 1071.

63. *Los Angeles Times* (June 4, 1916), pt. 2, 11 and (June 6, 1916), pt. 2, 1, and 5.

64. Richard H. Frost, *The Mooney Case* (Stanford, 1968), pp. 47–49.

65. *Assignment of Errors* (June 22, 1916), FRC-LA, RG 21, case 1071.

66. *Trial Record* (June 6, 1916), FRC-LA, RG 21, case 1071.

67. *Los Angeles Times* (June 6, 1916), pt. 2, 1, and 5.

68. Ibid. (June 7, 1916), pt. 2, 1, and 2. Oscar A. Trippet served as Indiana's youngest state senator and was first elected on the Prohibition ticket before moving to California. He entered law practice in San Diego, then Los Angeles, representing a number of large corporations before receiving President Wilson's appointment to the federal bench in 1915. William Andrew Spaulding, *History of Los Angeles City and County, California* (Los Angeles, 1931) 3: 31.

69. *Motion on Arrest of Judgment* (June 12, 1916), FRC-LA, RG 21, case 1071.

70. Judge Trippet's remarks are contained in *Bill of Exceptions* (September 20, 1916), FRC-LA, RG 21, case 1071. For Enrique's response see "Address of Enrique Flores Magón in the Federal Court, Los Angeles, June 22, 1916," *Mother Earth* (August 1916), pp. 570–578. Whether this was presented orally before the court has not been established. In any event it represented a major PLM statement.

71. Ibid.

72. *Court Record* (September 20, 1916), FRC-LA, RG 21, case 1071.

73. Mansel G. Gallaher to Attorney General (June 15, 1916), NA., RG 60, 90755.

74. *Los Angeles Times* (June 23, 1916), pt. 2, 8; *Court Record* (June 22, 1916) FRC-LA, RG 21, case 1071.

75. "Emma Goldman Has Been to Los Angeles!" *Mother Earth* (August 1916), pp. 591–592.

76. *Regeneración* (July 20, 1916).

77. *Bond of Ricardo Flores Magón* (June 24, 1916), FRC-LA, RG 21, case 1071.

78. *Bond of Ricardo Flores Magón* (July 1, 1916), FRC-LA, RG 21, case 1071.

79. "Emma Goldman Has Been to Los Angeles!" *Mother Earth* (August, 1916), pp. 591–592.

80. *Blast* (January 15, 1917), p. 6.

81. *Los Angeles Times* (July 15, 1916), pt. 2, 1; *Circular of Workers International Defense League* (July 1916), Special Collections, UCLA, collection 200. Pinchon coauthored the book with Lázaro Gutiérrez de Lara. Doubleday, Page, and Company published it in 1914.

82. Enrique Flores Magón to Dr. T. Perceval Gerson (August 24, 1916), Theodore Perceval Gerson Collection, Special Collections, UCLA, Collection 724, Box 2, file 4. Dr. Gerson, remembered as the father of the Hollywood Bowl, was extremely active in the political and cultural life in Southern California. A liberal sympathetic to the radical cause, he became director of the Southern California branch of the American Civil Liberties Union. The Severance Club was named after its oldest member Carolina Maria Seymour Severance (1820–1914), a pioneer in founding women's clubs, active in the abolitionist movement, women suffrage (being the first person to register in 1911 under California women suffrage law), interested in Christian socialism, progressivism, peace, and anti-imperialism. Emma Goldman, Max Eastman, Jane Addams, Upton Sinclair, and Clarence Darrow among others addressed the club members. Information concerning club activities is scattered throughout the Gerson papers.

83. A number of Mexican government officials toyed with the idea of offering Germany submarine bases, perhaps as a means of establishing a bargaining position with the United States and Britain. It is not clear to what extent the Zimmerman proposal (January 16, 1917) received serious consideration, either in Germany or Mexico. Carranza was aware of the danger of offering Wilson any pretext to intervene. P. Edward Haley, *Revolution and Intervention: The Diplomacy of Taft and Wilson with Mexico, 1910–1917* (Cambridge, Mass., 1970), pp. 248–253. Mark T. Gilderhus, *Diplomacy and Revolution: U.S.-Mexican Relations Under Wilson and Carranza* (Tucson, 1977), pp. 63–67.

84. *Los Angeles Times* (March 30, 1917), pt. 2, 1.

85. *Los Angeles Times* (April 24, 1917), pt. 2, 1; ibid. (April 29, 1917), pt. 2, 5; ibid. (May 8, 1917), pt. 1, 7.

86. "Magón et al. v. United States" (Circuit Court of Appeals, Ninth Circuit, February 4, 1918), *Federal Reporter* 248: 201–205.

87. "The Supreme Court refused to review the issue denying a petition for a writ of certiorari. "Enrique Flores Magón and Ricardo Flores Magón petitioners v. The United States of America, May 5, 1919," *Supreme Court Reporter* (November 1918–July 1919), 39: 391.

88. *Regeneración* (February 9, 1918); *Final Commitment of Enrique Flores Magón* (May 18, 1918), FRC-LA, RG 21, case 1071.

5: Los Angeles, 1918

1. Douglas W. Richmond, *Venustiano Carranza's Nationalist Struggle, 1893–1920* (Lincoln, 1983), pp. 127–132. Ramón Eduardo Ruíz, *The Great Rebellion: Mexico, 1905–1924* (New York, 1980), p. 210. Zapata attempted to recall Antonio I. Villarreal to his old liberal

principles in 1914. "Emiliano Zapata a General don Antonio I. Villa-rreal, Agosto 21 de 1914. Ramón Martínez Escamilla, *Emiliano Zapata: Escritos y Documentos* (Mexico, 1980), pp. 167–168.

2. The American Socialist Party doggedly resisted U.S. intervention and as a result, before the war ended every party official, including Eugene V. Debs, the perennial socialist presidential candidate, went to federal prison for anti-war activities. Many other socialists, such as Upton Sinclair, resigned from the party to support the war. The Department of Justice singled out the IWW for destruction because of their alleged addiction to industrial sabotage. Fear and hate substituted for evidence in order to sentence IWW officials to long sentences. The Chicago trial of the IWW leadership on the charge of conspiracy to violate wartime acts began April 1, 1918, the same month Flores Magón was indicted. Melvyn Dubovsky, *We Shall Be All: A History of the Industrial Workers of the World* (New York, 1969), pp. 423–437. For the condensed transcript of the trial see Harrison George, *The IWW Trial: Story of the Greatest Trial in Labor's History by One of the Defendants* (New York, 1969). Senator Harry Ashurst declared the IWW actually stood for "Imperial Wilhelm's Warriors," implying German backing. Philip Taft, "The Federal Trials of the IWW," *Labor History* (Winter 1962), p. 60. An interesting general view of this period is presented in Horace C. Peterson and Gilbert C. Fite, *Opponents of War, 1917–1918* (Madison, 1957). William Preston, Jr., *Aliens and Dissenters* (New York, 1966), pp. 105–106.

3. Harold M. Hyman, *To Try Men's Souls: Loyalty Tests in American History* (Berkeley, 1960), p. 271.

4. *New York Times* (December 26, 1917).

5. Ray Ginger, *The Bending Cross: A Biography of Eugene Victor Debs* (New Brunswick, 1949), p. 344.

6. David M. Kennedy, *Over Here: The First World War and American Society* (Oxford, 1980), p. 67.

7. Ibid., pp. 59, 77.

8. *Indictment in the District Court of the United States in and for the Southern District of California, Southern Division* (April 19, 1918), FRC-LA, RG 21, case 1421. The indictment charged violation of section 3 of title 1 and section 1 of title 12 of the Espionage Act of 1917, section 10 of the Trading with the Enemy Act, and section 211 of the Federal Penal Code of 1910 as amended.

9. "An Act to Punish Acts of Interference with the Foreign Relations, the Neutrality, and the Foreign Commerce of the United States, to Punish Espionage, and Better to Enforce the Criminal Laws of the United States, and for Other Purposes," *U.S. Statutes at Large*, 40: pt. 1, ch. 3, p. 219.

10. "An Act to Define, Regulate, and Punish Trading with the

Enemy, and for Other Purposes," *U.S. Statutes at Large*, 40: pt. 1, ch. 106, pp. 411–426.

11. *Post Office Annual Report for the Fiscal Year Ended June 30, 1918* (Washington, D.C., 1918), p. 13. In 1919 the Attorney General's office noted the existence of 222 radical newspapers published in a foreign language, 105 in English, and another 144 published in other countries, but received in this country for a total of 471. *Congressional Record: Proceedings and Debates*, 2nd session, 66th Congress. Deportation of Alien Anarchists (December 20, 1919), 59: pt. 1, p. 987. The emotional patriotism of the times did not receive the support of all academics. Professor Lindley M. Keasbey of the University of Texas, acknowledged by Walter Prescott Webb for providing the inspiration for his book, *The Great Plains*, was fired in 1917 for opposing the war. Others made similar sacrifices for their beliefs. William E. Nicholas, "World War I and Academic Dissent in Texas," *Arizona and the West* (Autumn 1972), p. 220.

12. *Indictment* (April 19, 1918). For the Spanish text of the manifesto see Armando Bartra, *Regeneración, 1900–1918: La corriente más radical de las revolución de 1910 a través de su periodico de combate* (Mexico, 1972), pp. 531–533.

13. Ibid.

14. *Demurrer* (April 29, 1918), FRC-LA, RG 21, case 1421.

15. Attempts to trace the background of jurors through the city directory proved unsatisfactory. Of those identified, many appeared to be in the insurance or real estate business.

16. Zechariah Chafee, Jr., *Free Speech in the United States* (Cambridge, Mass., 1948), p. 55.

17. United States v. Motion Picture Film, "The Spirit of '76," *Federal Reporter*, 252: series 1: p. 946.

18. For an interesting, if somewhat sentimental, account see Cornelius C. Smith, Jr., *Emilio Kosterlitzsky: Eagle of Sonora and the Southwest Border* (Glendale, Calif., 1970).

19. *Proposed Bill of Exceptions* (January 17, 1919), FRC-LA, RG 21, case 1421.

20. Ibid.

21. Ibid. *The Examiner* connected the PLM with wartime subversion headlining their story, "Magón put on Trial as Spy Law Violator," *Los Angeles Examiner* (July 16, 1918), pt. 1, 5.

22. *Los Angeles Times* (July 16, 1918), pt. 2, 8.

23. The rough draft of the circular of May 13, 1918, includes a discussion on the need to get an above-average lawyer, which, of course, required money to pay above-average fees. Unfortunately, the edited and finished circular did not include such a statement. Ryckman himself apparently indicated to Louis P. Lockner of the Liberty Defense Union that he himself did not expect remuneration.

Rough draft and the *Circular Letter* (May 13, 1918), copies at the Sherman Foundation Library, Corona del Mar. Nicholas Senn Zogg, son of the Netherlands consul in Mexico and a soldier of fortune who claimed to be a general in the Mexican army, worked with the PLM during the Baja invasion, and subsequently insisted that he had tricked Harry Chandler into financing arms purchases. Senn Zogg spent a term in Folsom Prison for passing a fifteen dollar bad check which he claimed was a frame-up. His activities continued to attract judicial attention. For sketchy details see the *Los Angeles Record* (May 15, 1917), pp. 1 and 6. Ethel Duffy Turner, *Ricardo Flores Magón y el Partido Liberal Mexicano* (Morelia, 1960), pp. 313–314.

24. Louis P. Locker, *Executive Committee of Liberty Defense Union to Defense Committee* (July 3, 1918), copy at the Sherman Foundation Library, Corona del Mar. David Starr Jordan had a strong interest in Mexican affairs. At the National Education Association meeting at the Hotel Astor in New York (July 7, 1916) he begged for understanding nonintervention, as well as indicated his somewhat reluctant support for Carranza. His address was published by the Mexican-American League under the title *What of Mexico?* (New York, 1916).

25. Guy Bogart to Nicholas Senn Zogg (July 4, 1918), copy at the Sherman Foundation Library, Corona del Mar. As the official organ of union labor the *Citizen* only mildly supported the Flores Magóns; however, it could be counted to be against American intervention in Mexico. See for example, "Labor Takes a Hand in Preventing War Being Made on Downtrodden Mexico: Here Are the Facts that Will Not Be Published in the Plutocratic Press," *Citizen* (July 21, 1916), p. 1. The *Citizen* supported Wilson and the war, using its influence to encourage Liberty Bond purchases.

26. *Los Angeles Times* (July 17, 1918), pt. 2, 1.

27. *Charge of the Court* (July 16, 1918), FRC-LA, RG 21, case 1421.

28. Ibid.

29. Ibid.

30. *Defense Instructions to the Jury* (July 16, 1918), FRC-LA, RG 21, case 1421.

31. *Verdict* (July 17, 1918), FRC-LA, RG 21, case 1421.

32. *Los Angeles Times* (July 20, 1918), pt. 2, 8.

33. *Judgement of the Court* (July 19, 1918), FRC-LA, RG 21, case 1421; *Los Angeles Times* (July 20, 1918), pt. 2, 8.

34. "Magón et al. v. United States, Circuit Court of Appeals, Ninth Circuit" (October 6, 1919), *Federal Reporter* 260: series 1 (November 1919–January 1920).

35. Ibid. The court cited as precedent *Mead v. United States*, 257 Fed. 639, 642, C.C.A.

36. *Los Angeles Times* (October 8, 1919), pt. 2, 5.

37. Hoover secured the ship from army authorities and invited select members of the House Immigration Committee to New York to see the radicals off. Max Lowenthal, *The Federal Bureau of Investigation* (New York, 1950), pp. 237–238. Richard Gid Powers, *Secrecy and Power: The Life of J. Edgar Hoover* (New York, 1987), pp. 74–89, provides a view of Hoover's manipulation of public opinion.

38. The *Times* in almost a nostalgic fashion reported Enrique's deportation under the heading "Magón Family Says Adios." *Los Angeles Times* (March 2, 1923), sec. 2, p. 9.

39. Max Lowenthal, pp. 135, 241. Created by Attorney General A. Mitchell Palmer, the GID regularly monitored radical newspapers and compiled files on individuals and organizations of alleged radical sympathies. Stanley Coben, *A. Mitchell Palmer: Politician* (New York, 1963), p. 207. The Attorney General's office reported that since the organization of the GID a "more or less complete history" of over 60,000 "radically inclined" individuals had been gathered together and classified, and a foundation for action laid either under the deportation acts or legislation to be enacted by Congress. *Congressional Record*, "Alien Anarchists," p. 987.

40. Samuel Kaplan, *Peleamos Contra La Injusticia: Enrique Flores Magón, Precursor De La Revolución Mexicana, Cuenta Su Historia a Samuel Kaplan* (Mexico, 1960), pp. 416–420. With considerable satisfaction Ambassador George T. Summerlin reported the arrest of Enrique Flores Magón in Mexico for attacking the Mexican government and the army before a crowd of 800 workmen. George T. Summerlin to Department of State (June 14, 1923), NA, State Department decimal file 312.1221.

6: Loose Ends: Los Angeles, 1918

1. Lucille Norman, according to her doctor, Carl Schultz, a sympathetic supporter as well as occasional bondsman for PLM members, became emotionally ill. In 1917 he served as Palma's surety and Lucille approached Dr. Gerson to be the other guarantor. In 1918, Palma went on trial falsely accused of murdering a grocer. Ricardo Flores Magón served as secretary-treasurer of the Raúl Palma defense Committee while Gerson became president. *Lucille Norman to Dr. T. Perceval Gerson* (May 31, 1917) and *Circular Letter of the Raúl Palma Defense Committee* (March 3, 1918), Theodore Perceval Gerson Collection, Special Collections, UCLA, 724, box 2, flds. 5, 6.

2. *Bench Warrant, United States District Court, Southern District of California* (July 12, 1918), Marshal's Criminal Docket no. 8385, FRC-LA, RG 21, case 1489.

3. *Indictment, United States District Court, Southern District of California* (July 12, 1918), FRC-LA, RG 21. The indictment charged

María with violation of Section 3, title 1 of the Espionage Act, section 19 of the Trading with the Enemy Act, and section 211 of the amended Federal Penal Code of 1910.

4. *Indictment* (July 12, 1918).

5. Ibid.

6. *Indictment, United States District Court, Southern District of California* (August 19, 1918), FRC-LA, RG 21, case 1508.

7. Ibid.

8. Ibid.

9. *Demurrer to Indictment, United States District Court, Southern District of California* (August 27, 1918), FRC-LA, RG 21, case 1508.

10. *Los Angeles Times* (October 8, 1918), pt. 2, 1.

11. *Bond to Appear, United States District Court, Southern District of California* (November 13, 1918), FRC-LA, RG 21, case 1508.

12. *Bond to Appear, United States District Court, Southern District of California* (November 12, 1918), FRC-LA, RG 21, case 1508.

13. *Letter of Authorization, Department of Justice to John R. O'Connor, United States Attorney, Los Angeles* (November 18, 1921), FRC-LA, RG 21, case 1508.

7: "HERE LIES A DREAMER": LEAVENWORTH FEDERAL PENITENTIARY, 1922

1. Palmer to F. H. Deuhay (September 6, 1918), Parole Rec., File 14596, Leavenworth, Bureau of Prisons, Washington, D.C.

2. Faced with legal action and adverse publicity the company negotiated a new contract. Lawrence A. Cardoso, *Mexican Emigration to the United States 1897–1931: Socio-Economic Patterns* (Tucson, 1980), p. 67.

3. Harry Schwartz, *Seasonal Farm Labor in the United States,* (New York, 1945), pp. 110–111; and Manuel P. Servín, "The Pre-World War II Mexican American," *California Historical Society Quarterly* (December 1966), pp. 325–338. The immigration act of 1917 allowed the Commissioner of Immigration to admit noneligible aliens on a temporary basis. On May 23, 1917, immigration authorities received orders to ignore the literacy test, head tax, and contract labor requirements in order to solve the agricultural manpower shortage in the Southwest. In June 1918 Mexican railroad section hands and coal miners were permitted legal entry. Farmer and others directly recruited their own labor force. George C. Kiser, "Mexican American Labor Before World War II," *Journal of Mexican American History* (Spring 1972), pp. 127–128.

4. Vernon H. Jenson, *Heritage of Conflict: Labor Relations in the Nonferrous Metals Industry up to 1930* (Ithica, 1950), p. 409.

5. Juan Gómez Quiñones, "The First Steps: Chicano Labor Conflict and Organizing, 1900–1920," *Aztlan* (Summer 1973), pp. 31–36.

6. Gilbert O'Day, "Ricardo Flores Magón," *The Nation* (December 2, 1922), pp. 689–690.

7. María Flores Magón to Dr. T. Perceval Gerson (n.d.), *Theodore Perceval Gerson Collection*, Special Collections, UCLA, 724, box 2, fld. 2/7. Located on a small island in southern Puget Sound, McNeil Island's cold and damp climate must have been disagreeable to Flores Magón, so accustomed to Southern California. A glimpse of life at McNeil is provided by Lester K. Price, *McNeil: A History of a Federal Prison* (McNeil, 1972).

8. Pandit to J. Robert O'Connor (September 4, 1918), NA., RG 60, 90755. Because of uncertainty whether a transfer would be beneficial, federal authorities did not authorize a special transfer, but advised Flores Magón's inclusion in the next general shipment of convicts to Kansas.

9. Librado Rivera to Raúl Palma (November 25, 1922) in Juan Gómez-Quiñones, *Sembradores Ricardo Flores Magón y el Partido Liberal Mexicano: A Eulogy and Critique* (Los Angeles, 1973), pp. 154–155. Bill Haywood also suffered from diabetes while at Leavenworth, and complained of failing eyesight. Eventually he suffered a paralytic stroke in Moscow. William D. Haywood, *Bill Haywood's Book: The Autobiography of William D. Haywood* (New York, 1929), p. 332, 362, 365.

10. Ricardo Flores Magón to Emma Barsky (March 16, 1922) and to Ellen White (Lilly Sarnoff) (August 25, 1922) in Gómez-Quiñones, *Sembradores*, pp. 150–151 and 153–154.

11. Kate Crane Gartz to Margaret Wilson (n.d.) in *Parlor Provocateur: From Salon to Soapbox* (Pasadena, 1923), pp. 33–34.

12. Ricardo Flores Magón to Nicolás Bernal (December 6, 1920) in Ricardo Flores Magón, *Vida y Obra* (Mexico 1923–1925), 4: 16, 23–24.

13. Ricardo Flores Magón, to Nicolás Bernal (December 20, 1921) in Ricardo Flores Magón, *Epistolario revolucionario e intimo* (Mexico, D.F., 1925), 1: 30–33.

14. Ricardo Flores Magón to Ellen White (Lilly Sarnoff) (June 28, 1921) in *Vida y Obra*, 6: 23–24.

15. Ralph Chaplin, *Wobbly* (Chicago, 1948), p. 225. Bill Haywood described prison life at Leavenworth in 1918–1919. Haywood, pp. 327–338. Haywood left Leavenworth in July 1919, several months before Flores Magón's arrival.

16. Ibid., p. 310.

17. Richard Drinnon, *Rebel in Paradise: A Biography of Emma Goldman* (Chicago, 1961), p. 198.

18. See the remarks by Congressman Albert Johnson of Wash-

ington concerning Weinberger's defense of "Class-war prisoners."
Congressional Record: Appendix of Proceedings and Debates, 2nd session,
66th Congress. Extension of Remarks of Hon. Albert Johnson (June
3, 1920), 59: pt. 9, p. 9279. A recent example is provided by the interesting career of Attorney William Kunstler, well known for his
defense of the Chicago Seven and other radical causes, as well as
the civil-rights movement.

19. Quoted in Juan Gómez-Quiñones, *Sembradores,* p. 147.

20. Quoted in Peterson and Fite, *Opponents of War, 1917–1918,*
p. 271.

21. *Congressional Record: Proceedings and Debates,* 67th Cong. 4th
session (December 14, 1922), p. 488. As late as June 1923 the government attempted to secure a show of repentance from political prisoners. President Harding offered to free twenty-four Leavenworth
IWWs in return for their promise to be "law-abiding." A number of
them declined on the ground that it constituted an admission of
guilt. Finally, in December 1923, President Coolidge freed all political prisoners. Senator Borah congratulated Coolidge on his discovery of the first amendment of the U.S. Constitution. Peterson and
Fite, *Opponents of War,* pp. 283–284.

22. Ricardo Flores Magón to Nicolás Bernal (December 6, 1920),
Epistolario revolucionario, I, 23–24.

23 Ralph Chaplin, *Wobbly,* p. 310.

24. Ethel Duffy Turner, *Ricardo Flores Magón y el Partido Liberal
Mexicano,* p. 338. Enrique believed he had been strangled and the
story of a heart failure was totally out of the question since no mention had been made earlier of heart problems. Samuel Kaplan, *Combatimos la Tirania* (Mexico, 1958), p. 320.

25. Medical research conducted by Professor Edward Arguilla, a
pathologist at the University of California, Irvine medical school,
demonstrated the wide effects of diabetes, and its little-recognized
connection with heart attacks. "Diabetes Death Higher than Figures
Show," *Los Angeles Times* (June 8, 1975), pt. 2, 3. Raat, advised by
Charles B. Mosher, M.D., discounts the idea of diabetes. W. Dirk
Raat, *Revoltosos: Mexico's Rebels in the United States, 1903–1923* (College Station, 1981), p. 287. Bureau of Prisons–Leavenworth Penitentiary, file 14596.

26. Ethel Duffy Turner, *Ricardo Flores Magón,* p. 342.

27. *Debs Magazine* (December 1922), p. 15. Debs described his
own experience in Atlanta Federal Penitentiary, including his stay
in the hospital because of weight loss and "weak heart action" in
Eugene Victor Debs, *Walls and Bars* (Chicago, 1927).

28. Kate Crane Gartz to President Warren G. Harding (December
18, 1922), *Parlor Provocateur,* p. 100.

29. Quoted in Peterson and Fite, *Opponents of War,* p. 282.

30. *Debs Magazine* (January 1923), p. 10.
31. Quoted in Paul Avrich, *Anarchist Portraits* (Princeton, 1988), p. 212.
32. *Congressional Record; Proceedings and Debates*, 4th session, 67th Congress. Remarks of Mr. Lineberger concerning Ricardo Flores Magón (December 11, 1922), 64: pt. 1, p. 299.
33. *Los Angeles Times* (November 22, 1922), pt. 2, 1.
34. For the complete text see Ricardo Flores Magón, *Tribuna roja* (Mexico, 1925), pp. 5–11.
35. Ethel Duffy Turner, *Ricardo Flores Magón*, pp. 325–333.
36. John W. F. Dulles, *Yesterday in Mexico: A Chronicle of the Revolution, 1919–1936* (Austin, 1961), p. 278.
37. John Q. Wood, American Consulate, Veracruz to Department of State (November 20, 1922); James B. Stewart, American Consulate, Tampico to Department of State (January 8, 1922), NA., State Department Decimal file 311.1221.
38. The contradictions in Obregón's revolutionary rhetoric could not stand the slightest examination. For example, his public position on land reform recalled that of Francisco Madero in that it appeared to promise protection of private property rights while providing for the creation of small holdings. Ramón Eduardo Ruíz, *The Great Rebellion, Mexico, 1905–1924* (New York, 1980), pp. 313–322.
39. Cardoso, *Mexican Immigration to the U.S.*, pp. 102–103.
40. While critical, returnees were not ready to overthrow the government. The broadening experience, however, gave many of them their first means of comparison. For a view of the process see María Herrera-Sobek, *The Bracero Experience: Elitelore versus Folklore* (Los Angeles, 1979), pp. 121–128. Primo Tapia, who returned to Mexico in 1920 to lead his village in the struggle for agrarian reform, was an exception. He had joined Ricardo Flores Magón in Los Angeles and with Ricardo's help attended night school. Subsequently, Primo became an IWW organizer and traveled throughout the United States. Paul Friedrich, *Agrarian Revolt in a Mexican Village* (Englewood Cliffs, N.J., 1970), pp. 64–70.
41. The United States finally recognized the Obregón regime in August 1923. Narcisco Bassoles Batalla, *El Pensamiento Politico de Alvaro Obregón* (Mexico, 1967), p. 58. Charles Dennis Ignasias, "Reluctant Recognition: The United States and the Recognition of Alvaro Obregón of Mexico, 1920–1924" (Ph.D. diss., Michigan State University, 1967), pp. 115, 122.
42. Philip S. Foner, ed., *Mother Jones Speaks: Collected Writings and Speeches* (New York, 1983), pp. 528–530. Edward M. Steel, ed., *The Correspondence of Mother Jones* (Pittsburgh, 1985), p. xxxv.
43. Harry Weinberger, "Two Political Prisoners at Leavenworth," *The New Republic* (July 5, 1922), p. 162.

44. Kate Crane Gartz to Attorney General Daugherty (July 25, 1922), *Parlor Provocateur*, pp. 88–89.

45. NA., Group 59, State Department Decimal file 311.1221. Librado Rivera, after his release in October 1923, returned to Mexico to agitate amongst the Tampico petroleum workers and publish *Avante!*, a weekly, which resulted in his confinement in Andomegui Penitentiary. Ethel Duffy Turner, *Ricardo Flores Magón*, p. 359.

46. *Los Angeles Times* (November 27, 1922), pt. 1,1.

8: THE LIMITS OF FREEDOM

1. Servín aptly characterized the Mexican-American as the most ignored historically of all ethnic minorities in the United States. Manuel P. Servín, ed., *The Mexican Americans: An Awakening Minority* (Beverly Hills, 1970), p. vii.

2. Paul Avrich, *Anarchist Portraits* (Princeton, 1988), p. 165.

3. See for example her curt dismissal of Frank Tannenbaum's contributions after his release from Blackwell's Island. Elizabeth Gurley Flynn, *I Speak My Own Piece: Autobiography of the "Rebel Girl"* (New York, 1955), pp. 167, 169.

4. Walter Fogel, *Mexican Illegal Alien Workers in the United States* (Los Angeles, 1978) presents some preliminary findings on the topic.

5. The symbiotic relation between the Southwest and northern Mexico is demonstrated in Niles Hanson, *The Border Economy: Regional Development in the Southwest* (Austin, 1981).

6. Eduardo Blanquel, "El Anarco-Magónismo," *Historia Mexicana* (Enero–Marzo, 1964), p. 403.

7. A wealthy woman, Mabel Dodge, established her salon in New York City after returning from Florence, Italy, in 1912. More "radical chic" than philosophical in her interests, her salon attracted Big Bill Haywood of the IWW, John Reed, Frank Tannenbaum, Emma Goldman, Alexander Berkman, Max Eastman, Walter Lippman, as well as many other radicals and nonconformists. She captured the flavor of her salon in various autobiographical works, especially in Mabel Dodge Luhan, *Movers and Shakers* (New York, 1936).

8. There is some indication that even after doubts concerning the guilt of Sacco and Vanzetti had became widespread, public opinion demanded that "they ought to be hung anyway." Quoted in Marion Denman Frankfurter and Gardner Jackson, eds. *The Letters of Sacco and Vanzetti* (New York, 1928), p. x. For Vanzetti's comments on Flores Magón see p. 169.

9. *United States Code Annotated*, "Crimes and Criminal Procedure," title 18, ch. 71, "Obscenity," p. 1461. In a more recent inci-

dent the Trading with the Enemy Act of 1917, used against Flores Magón, came to life when the Treasury Department blocked the delivery of 30,000 copies of a Cuban journal addressed to individuals in the United States under the provisions of the act. *New York Times* (July 6, 1981), p. 4.

10. A discussion of Holmes's intellectual process is contained in Richard Polenberg, *Fighting Faiths: The Abrams Case, The Supreme Court, and Free Speech* (New York, 1987), pp. 236–242.

Works Cited

ARCHIVAL AND DOCUMENTARY COLLECTIONS

Los Angeles Federal Records Center, Laguna Hills, California.
John Murray Collection and the Silvestre Terrazas Collection. Bancroft Library, University of California, Berkeley, California.
National Archives. Washington, D.C.
Sherman Foundation. Corona del Mar, California.
Theodore Perceval Gerson Collection and the Oral History Project. Special Collections, UCLA. Los Angeles, California.

NEWSPAPERS AND PERIODICALS

American Federationist
Appeal to Reason
Blast
The Citizen
Debs Magazine
International Socialist Review
Los Angeles Examiner
Los Angeles Herald
Los Angeles Times
Miner's Magazine
Mother Earth
The Nation
The New Republic
New York Call
New York Times
Regeneración
Tucson Citizen
Why?
Wilshire's Magazine

U.S. STATUTES

"An Act to Amend Section 211 *Federal Penal Code of 1910*." *U.S. Statutes at Large*, 61st Congress, *1909–1911*, 36: pt. 1, p. 1339.

"An Act to Define, Regulate, and Punish Trading with the Enemy, and for other Purposes." *U.S. Statutes at Large,* 40: pt. 1, ch. 106, pp. 411–425.

"An Act to Punish Acts of Interference with the Foreign Relations, the Neutrality, and the Foreign Commerce of the United States, to Punish Espionage, and Better to Enforce the Criminal Laws of the United States, and for other Purposes." *U.S. Statutes at Large,* 40: pt. 1, ch. 3, p. 219.

OTHER SOURCES

Aguirre, Norberto. *Ricardo Flores Magón, síntesis biográfica.* Mexico, 1964.

Albro, Ward Sloan. "Ricardo Flores Magón and the Liberal Party: An Inquiry into the Origins of the Mexican Revolution of 1910." Ph.D. diss., University of Arizona, 1967.

Anderson, Rodney D. *Outcasts in Their Own Land: Mexican Industrial Workers, 1906–1911.* DeKalb, 1976.

Annual Report of the Postmaster General for the Fiscal Year Ended June 30, 1918. Washington, D.C., 1918.

Aparicio, Alfonso López. *El movimiento obrero en Mexico: antecedents, desarrollo y tendencias.* Mexico, 1952.

Avrich, Paul. *An American Anarchist: The Life of Voltairine de Cleyre.* Princeton, 1978.

————. *Anarchist Portraits.* Princeton, 1988.

————, ed. "Prison Letters of Ricardo Flores Magón to Lilly Sarnoff," *International Review of Social History,* 1977, pp. 379–422.

Barrera Fuentes, Florencia. *Historia de la revolución Mexicana, la etapa precursora.* Mexico, 1955.

Barta, Armando, "La Otra Revolución Mexicana." *Siempre,* Diciembre 20, 1972. Suplemento 2–6.

————. *Regeneración, 1910–1918: La corriente más radical de la revolución de 1910 a través de su periodico de combate.* Mexico, 1972.

Batalla, Narcisso Bassales. *El Pensamiento Político de Alvaro Obregón.* Mexico, 1967.

Beezley, William H. *Insurgent Governor: Abraham González and the Mexican Revolution in Chihuahua.* Lincoln, 1973.

Beltrán, Gonzálo Aguirre, ed. *Ricardo Flores Magón, Antologia.* Mexico, 1970.

Bernal, Nicolás T., ed. *Ricardo Flores Magón: Vida y Obra.* 10 vols. Mexico, 1923–1925.

Bernstein, Marvin D. *The Mexican Mining Industry 1890–1950: A Study of the Interaction of Politics, Economics, and Technology.* Albany, 1965.

Blaisdell, Lowell L. "Harry Chandler and Mexican Border Intrigue, 1914–1917." *Pacific Historical Review,* November 1966, pp. 385–393.

————. *The Desert Revolution, Baja California, 1911.* Madison, 1962.

Blanquel, Eduardo. "El Anarco-Magónismo." *Historia Mexicana,* Enero–Marzo, 1964, pp. 394–427.

Brophy, Blake A. *Foundlings on the Frontier: Racial and Religious Conflict in Arizona Territory, 1904–1905.* Tucson, 1972.

Brown, Lyle C. "The Mexican Liberals and Their Struggle against the Díaz Dictatorship: 1900–1906." *Antologia Mexico City College.* Mexico, 1956, pp. 317–362.

Bureau of Prisons–Leavenworth Penitentiary, file 14596.

Cadenhead, Ivie E., Jr. "The American Socialists and the Mexican Revolution of 1910." *Southwestern Social Science Quarterly,* September 1962, pp. 103–117.

Callahan, James Morton. *American Foreign Policy in Mexican Relations.* New York, 1967.

Cánovas, Agustín Cúe. *Ricardo Flores Magón, la Baja California y los Estados Unidos.* Mexico, 1957.

Cardoso, Lawrence A. *Mexican Emigration to the United States 1897–1931: Socio-Economic Patterns.* Tucson, 1980.

Carr, Barry. *El movimiento obrero y la politíca en México, 1910–1929.* 2 vols. Mexico, 1976.

Chafee, Zechariah, Jr. *Free Speech in the United States.* Cambridge, Mass., 1948.

Chaplin, Ralph. *Wobbly.* Chicago, 1948.

Christopulos, Diana K. "American Radicals and the Mexican Revolution, 1900–1925." Ph.D. diss., State University of New York at Binghamton, 1980.

Circuit Court of Appeals. "Magón et al. v. United States." *Federal Reporter,* 248: Series 1, 201–205.

————. "Magón et al. v. United States." *Federal Reporter,* 260: Series 1, 811–814.

————. "United States v. Motion Picture Film, 'The Spirit of '76.'" *Federal Reporter,* 252: Series 1, pp. 946–948.

Clark, Marjorie, Ruth. *Organized Labor in Mexico.* Chapel Hill, 1934.

Cleyre, Voltairine de. "The Mexican Revolution." *Mother Earth.* December 1911, January and February 1912, pp. 301–306, 335–341, and 374–380.

Coben, Stanley. *A. Mitchell Palmer: Politician.* New York, 1963.

Cockcroft, James D. *Intellectual Precursors of the Mexican Revolution, 1900–1913.* Austin, 1968.

Congressional Record: Appendix of Proceedings and Debates. 2nd Session, 66th Congress. Extension of Remarks of Hon. Albert Johnson, June 3, 1920 concerning radicals. V. 59: pt. 9, pp. 9278–9280.

Congressional Record: Proceedings and Debates. 2nd Session, 66th Congress. Deportation of Alien Anarchists, December 20, 1919. 59: pt. 1, pp. 983–989.

————. 4th session, 67th Congress. Remarks of Mr. Lineberger, December 11, 1922 concerning Ricardo Flores Magón. 69: pt. 1, pp. 298–300, 488.

Conlin, Joseph R. *Big Bill Haywood and the Radical Union Movement.* Syracuse, 1969.

Cumberland, Charles C. "Border Raids in the Lower Rio Grande Valley—1915." *Southern Historical Quarterly,* January 1954, p. 285–311.

Daniel, Cletus E. *Bitter Harvest: A History of California Farm Workers, 1870–1941.* Ithaca, 1981.

Debs, Eugene Victor. "This Plot Must Be Foiled." *Appeal to Reason,* October 10, 1908.

———. *Walls and Bars.* New York, 1973.

———. *Writings and Speeches of Eugene V. Debs.* New York, 1948.

———. "You Will Reap the Whirlwind." *Appeal to Reason.* November 6, 1909, p. 4.

Dolsen, Ethel. "Mexican Revolutionist in the United States." *Miner's Magazine,* June 11, 1908, pp. 6–10.

Drinnon, Richard. *Rebel in Paradise: A Biography of Emma Goldman.* Chicago, 1961.

Dubofsky, Melvyn. *We Shall Be All: A History of the Industrial Workers of the World.* New York, 1969.

Dulles, John W. F. *Anarchists and Communists in Brazil, 1900–1935.* Austin, 1973.

———. *Yesterday in Mexico: A Chronicle of the Revolution, 1919–1936.* Austin, 1961.

Escobar, Edward J. "Mexican Revolutionaries and the Los Angeles Police: Harassment of the Partido Liberal Mexicano, 1907–1910." *Aztlan,* Spring 1986, pp. 1–46.

Estrada, Leobardo F., et al. "Chicanos in the United States: A History of Exploitation and Resistance." *Daedalus,* Spring 1981, pp. 103–131.

Fabela, Isidro and Josefina E., eds. *Documentos historicos de la Revolución Mexicana.* 28 vols. Mexico, 1960–1976.

Federal Penal Code in Force, January 1, 1910. Boston, 1910.

Fetherling, Dale. *Mother Jones, the Miners' Angel: A Portrait.* Carbondale, 1974.

Fine, Sidney. "Anarchism and the Assassination of McKinley." *American Historical Review,* July 1955.

Flores Magón, Ricardo. "The Appeal of Mexico to American Labor." *Mother Earth,* April 1911, pp. 47–49.

Flynn, Elizabeth Gurley. *I Speak My Own Piece: Autobiography of the "Rebel Girl."* New York, 1955.

Fogel, Walter. *Mexican Illegal Alien Workers in the United States.* Los Angeles, 1978.

Foner, Philip S. *History of the Labor Movement in the United States*. 5 vols. New York, 1947–1980.
―――. *The Industrial Workers of the World, 1905–1917*. New York, 1965.
Frankfurter, Marion Denman and Gardner Jackson, eds. *The Letters of Sacco and Vanzetti*.
Friedrich, Paul. *Agrarian Revolt in a Mexican Village*. Englewood Cliffs, N.J., 1970.
Frost, Richard H. *The Mooney Case*. Stanford, 1968.
Furlong, Thomas. *Fifty Years a Detective*. St. Louis, 1912.
García, Mario T. *Desert Immigrants: The Mexicans of El Paso, 1880–1920*. New Haven, 1981.
Gartz, Kate Crane. *Parlor Provocateur or from Salon to Soapbox*. Pasadena, 1923.
George, Harrison. *The IWW Trial: Story of the Greatest Trial in Labor's History by One of the Defendants*. New York, 1969.
Gilderhus, Mark T. *Diplomacy and Revolution: U.S. Mexican Relations Under Wilson and Carranza*. Tucson, 1977.
Ginger, Ray. *The Bending Cross: A Biography of Eugene Victor Debs*. New Brunswick, 1949.
Goldman, Emma. *Anarchism and Other Essays*. New York, 1911.
Goldstein, Robert Justin. *Political Repression in Modern America from 1870 to the Present*. Cambridge, Mass., 1978.
Gompers, Samuel. *President Gompers Presents the Case of the Imprisoned Mexican Patriots to President Roosevelt*. Chicago, 1909.
―――. *Seventy Years of Life and Labour*. 2 vols. New York, 1925.
―――. "United States-Mexico-Labor-Their Relations." *American Federationist*, August 1916, pp. 633–651.
González Ramírez, Manuel. *Fuentes para la historia de la Revolución Mexicana*. 4 vols. Mexico, 1954–1957.
―――, ed. *Epistolario y textos de Ricardo Flores Magón*. Mexico, 1964.
Haley, P. Edward. *Revolution and Intervention: The Diplomacy of Taft and Wilson with Mexico, 1910–1917*. Cambridge, Mass., 1973.
Hall, Linda B. *Alvaro Obregón: Power and Revolution in Mexico, 1911–1920*. College Station, 1981.
Hanlen, Charles Jacob. "Ricardo Flores Magón: Biography of a Revolutionary." M.A. thesis, University of San Diego, 1967.
Hansen, Niles. *The Border Economy: Regional Development in the Southwest*. Austin, 1981.
Harris, Charles H., and Louis R. Sadler. *The Border and the Revolution*. Las Cruces, 1988.
―――. "The Plan of San Diego and the Mexican–United States War Crisis of 1916: A Reexamination." *Hispanic American Historical Review*, August, 1978, pp. 381–408.

Hart, John M. *Anarchism and the Mexican Working Class, 1860–1931.* Austin, 1978.

———. *Los Anarquistas Mexicanos, 1860–1900.* Mexico, 1974.

———. *Revolutionary Mexico: The Coming and Process of the Mexican Revolution.* Berkeley, 1987.

Haywood, William D. *Bill Haywood's Book: The Autobiography of William D. Haywood.* New York, 1929.

Hernández, Salvador. *Magonismo y Movimiento Obrero en Mexico: Cananea y Río Blanco.* Mexico, 1977.

Herrera-Sobek, María. *The Bracero Experience: Elitelore versus Folklore.* Los Angeles, 1979.

Hunt, Rockwell D. *California and Californians.* 3 vols. Los Angeles, 1930.

Hyman, Harold M. *To Try Men's Souls: Loyalty Tests in American History.* Berkeley, 1960.

Ignasias, Charles Dennis. "Reluctant Recognition: The United States and the Recognition of Alvaro Obregón of Mexico, 1920–1924." Ph.D. diss., Michigan State University, 1967.

Ireland, Robert E. "The Radical Community, Mexican and American Radicalism, 1900–1910." *Journal of Mexican American History,* Fall 1971, pp. 22–32.

Jenson, Vernon H. *Heritage of Conflict: Labor Relations in the Nonferrous Metals Industries up to 1930.* Ithaca, 1950.

Joll, James. *The Anarchists.* New York, 1966.

Jones, Mary Harris. *Autobiography of Mother Jones.* New York, 1969.

Jordan, David Starr. *What of Mexico?* New York, 1916.

Kaplan, Samuel. *Combatimos la tiranía: "Conversaciones con Enrique Flores Magón."* Mexico, 1958.

———. *Peleamos Contra la Injusticia: Enrique Flores Magón, Precursor de la Revolución Mexicana, Cuenta su Historia a Samuel Kaplan.* Mexico, 1960.

Kennedy, David M. *Birth Control in America.* New Haven, 1970.

———. *Over Here: The First World War and American Society.* Oxford, 1980.

Kerig, Dorothy Pierson. *Luther T. Ellsworth, U.S. Consul on the Border During the Mexican Revolution.* El Paso, 1975.

Kiser, George C. "Mexican American Labor Before World War II." *Journal of Mexican American History,* Spring 1972, pp. 122–137.

Knight, Alan. *The Mexican Revolution.* 2 vols. Cambridge, 1986.

La France, David G. *The Mexican Revolution in Puebla, 1908–1913: The Maderista Movement and the Failure of Liberal Reform.* Wilmington, Del., 1989.

Langham, Thomas C. *Border Trials; Ricardo Flores Magón and the Mexican Liberals.* El Paso, 1981.

Lawler, Oscar. "Oral History Interview." Oral History Project. UCLA. Los Angeles, 1962.

Levenstein, Harvey A. *Labor Organizations in the United States and Mexico: A History of Their Relations*. Westport, 1971.

Lingenfelter, Richard E. *The Hardrock Miners: A History of the Mining Labor Movement in the West, 1863–1893*. Berkeley, 1974.

Lowenthal, Max. *The Federal Bureau of Investigation*. New York, 1950.

Luhan, Mabel Dodge. *Movers and Shakers*. New York, 1936.

Martínez Escamilla, Ramón. *Emiliano Zapata: Escritos y Documentos*. Mexico, 1980.

Mellon, Knox, Jr. "Job Harriman: The Early and Middle Years, 1861–1912." Ph.D. diss., Claremont Graduate School, 1972.

Meyer, Michael D. *Huerta: A Political Portrait*. Lincoln, 1972.

Meyers, Ellen Howell. "The Mexican Liberal Party, 1903–1910." Ph.D. diss., University of Virginia, 1971.

Miller, Richard N. "American Railroad Unions and the National Railways of Mexico: An Exercise in Nineteenth-Century Proletarian Manifest Destiny." *Labor History*, Spring 1974, pp. 239–260.

Nettlau, Max. *Historia de la Anarquia*. Barcelona, 1978.

Nicholas, William E. "World War I and Academic Dissent in Texas." *Arizona and the West*, Autumn 1972, pp. 215–230.

O'Day, Gilbert. "Ricardo Flores Magón." *The Nation*, December 2, 1922, pp. 684–690.

Owen, William C. "Mexico and Socialism." *Mother Earth*, September 1911, pp. 199–202.

———. "Mexico's Hour of Need." *Mother Earth*, June 1911, pp. 105–107.

———. "The Death of Ricardo Flores Magón." Reprinted from *Freedom*, December 1922 in David Poole, ed., *Land and Liberty: Anarchist Influence in the Mexican Revolution—Ricardo Flores Magón*. Sanday, Orkney, 1977.

———. "Viva Mexico." *Mother Earth*, April 1911, pp. 42–46.

Parlee, Lorena M. "The Impact of United States Railroad Unions on Organized Labor and Government Policy in Mexico (1880–1911)." *Hispanic American Historical Review*, August, 1984, pp. 443–475.

Peterson, Horace C., and Gilbert C. Fite. *Opponents of War, 1917–1918*. Madison, 1957.

Pinchon, Edgcomb. "Think of the Magóns." *Blast*, June 1, 1916, p. 1.

Pletcher, David M. *Rails, Mines, and Progress: Seven American Promoters in Mexico, 1867–1911*. Ithaca, 1958.

Polenberg, Richard. *Fighting Faiths: The Abrams Case, The Supreme Court, and Free Speech*. New York, 1987.

Post Office Department Annual Report for Fiscal Year Ended June 30, 1919. Washington, D.C., 1919.

Powers, Richard Gid. *Secrecy and Power: The Life of J. Edgar Hoover.* New York, 1987.

Preston, William, Jr. *Aliens and Dissenters.* New York, 1966.

Price, Lester K. *McNeil: History of a Federal Prison.* McNeil, 1972.

Quiñones, Juan Gómez. "The First Steps: Chicano Labor Conflict and Organizing, 1900–1920." *Aztlán,* Summer 1973, pp. 31–36.

———. "Plan de San Diego Reviewed." *Aztlán,* Spring 1970.

———. *Sembradores: Ricardo Flores Magón y El Partido Liberal Mexicano: A Eulogy and Critique.* Los Angeles, 1973.

Raat, W. Dirk. "The Diplomacy of Suppression; Los Revoltosos, Mexico and the United States, 1906–1911." *Hispanic American Historical Review,* November 1976, pp. 529–550.

———. *Revoltosos: Mexico's Rebels in the United States, 1903–1923.* College Station, 1981.

Radosh, Ronald. *American Labor and United States Foreign Policy.* New York, 1969.

Reichert, William O. *Partisans of Freedom: A Study in American Anarchism.* Bowling Green, Ohio, 1976.

Renshaw, Patrick. *The Wobblies: The Story of Syndicalism in the United States.* New York, 1968.

Richmond, Douglas W. *Venustiano Carranza's Nationalist Struggle, 1893–1920.* Lincoln, 1983.

Ross, Stanley R. *Francisco I. Madero: Apostle of Mexican Democracy.* New York, 1955.

Ruíz, Ramón Eduardo. *The Great Rebellion, Mexico 1905–1924.* New York, 1980.

Sandos, James A. "The Plan of San Diego: War and Diplomacy on the Texas Border." *Arizona and the West,* Spring 1972, pp. 5–24.

Santillán, Diego Abad de. *Ricardo Flores Magón, el apostol de la revolución social Mexicana.* Mexico, 1925.

Schwartz, Harry. *Seasonal Farm Labor in the United States.* New York, 1945.

Senate Documents, 66th Congress. 2d Session, 1919–1920. *Investigation of Mexican Affairs,* 2 vols. Washington, D.C., 1920.

Servín, Manuel P. "The Pre-World War II Mexican American." *California Historical Society Quarterly,* December 1966, pp. 325–338.

———, ed. *The Mexican Americans: An Awakening Minority.* Beverly Hills, 1970.

Shannon, David A. *The Socialist Party of America: A History.* New York, 1955.

Smith, Cornelius C., Jr. *Emilio Kosterlitzky: Eagle of Sonora and the Southwest Border.* Glendale, 1970.

Snow, Sinclair. *The Pan-American Federation of Labor.* Durham, 1964.

Sonnichsen, C. L. *Colonel Green and the Copper Skyrocket.* Tucson, 1974.

Spalding, William Andrew. *History of Los Angeles City and County, California.* 3 vols. Los Angeles, 1931.

Stanford, Leland G. *Footprints of Justice in San Diego and Profiles of Senior Members of the Bench and Bar.* San Diego, 1960.

Steel, Edward M., ed. *The Correspondence of Mother Jones.* Pittsburgh, 1985.

―――. *The Speeches and Writings of Mother Jones.* Pittsburgh, 1988.

Steffens, Lincoln. *The Autobiography of Lincoln Steffens.* New York, 1931.

Stimson, Grace H. *The Rise of the Labor Movement in Los Angeles.* Berkeley, 1955.

Taft, Philip. "The Federal Trials of the IWW" *Labor History,* Winter 1962, pp. 57–91.

Trowbridge, Elizabeth D. *Political Prisoners Held in the United States: Refugees Imprisoned at the Request of a Foreign Government.* N.p., n.d.

Turner, Ethel Duffy. *Revolution in Baja California: Ricardo Flores Magón's High Noon.* Edited and Annotated by Rey Devis. Detroit, 1981.

―――. *Ricardo Flores Magón y el Partido Liberal Mexicano.* Morelia, 1960.

Turner, John Kenneth. "Anti-Jingoes Win an Epoch-Making Victory; Why Wilson Turns Back from Mexican War." *Appeal to Reason,* July 22, 1916, p. 1.

United States House of Representatives. *Hearing on the House Joint Resolution 210 Providing for Joint Committee to Investigate Alleged Persecution of Mexican Citizens by the Government of Mexico.* Washington, D.C., 1910.

―――. *Resolution: Requesting Information of the Attorney General Concerning the Imprisonment of Certain Persons at Florence, Arizona.* Washington, D.C., 1910.

United States Supreme Court. "Enrique Flores Magón and Ricardo Flores Magón petitioners v. United States of America, May 5, 1919." *Supreme Court Reporter,* November 1918–July 1919, 39: 391.

Vanderwood, Paul J. *Disorder and Progress: Bandits, Police, and Mexican Development.* Lincoln, 1981.

Weinberger, Harry. "Two Political Prisoners at Leavenworth." *The New Republic,* July 5, 1922, p. 162.

Weintraub, Hyman. "The I.W.W. in California, 1905–1931." M.A. thesis, University of California, Los Angeles, 1947.

Womack, John, Jr. *Zapata and the Mexican Revolution.* New York, 1969.

Index

Addams, Jane: as treasurer of Mexican Political Refugee Committee, 23

Alexander, Joseph L. B.: opinion of Arizona conspiracy trial, 21; links PLM with anarchism, 26; obtains conviction of PLM in Tucson, 29

Anarchism: defined, 6; secret commitment to of PLM, 6; stereotype of, 7; association of with immigrants, 7; fear of in 1906, 14; laws against, 15; incidents in 1908 attributed to, 26; ambivalent approach of to violence, 39; emotional assessment of in 1916 proceedings, 67; events associated with in 1914 and 1915, 68; use of Thomas Jefferson to demonstrate native roots of, 70; emotional assessment of in 1918 proceedings, 86; Flores Magón in the context of the failure of, 111; public support of rigged trials of, 116

Andrews, Willedd: arguments of in 1912 proceedings, 45, 46

Appeal to Reason: front page article (1909) of in defenses of PLM leaders, 24; blamed for threatening letter, 25; linkage of PLM with international revolutionary movement by, 27; publicity of in favor of non-intervention, 34; telegram to from Mother Jones, 36; attitude of toward Madero, 37

Australia: manifesto and *Regeneración* sent to, 42

Baja California: why selected for armed attack on, 34; plan of attack on, 35

Baltimore Sun: comments of on Flores Magón's death, 104

Berkman, Alexander: approach of to violence, 39; comments of on PLM 1916 indictment, 62, 63; support of for Flores Magón in 1916 proceedings, 65; praise of for Flores Magón, 67; refers to Flores Magón as the Kropotkin of Mexico, 72; noted, 111

Blackwell, Alice Stone: noted, 116

Bledsoe, Benjamin F.: remarks of on anarchism and the law, 87; on section 211 of Penal Code, 88; orders arrest of María Flores Magón, 93

Bonaparte, Charles J.: warning of concerning illegal deportations, 26

Border: economic integration of, 11; Gomper's view of, 12; political atmosphere of in 1906, 14; President Roosevelt alerts War Department of possible danger of, 17; concern over radical contamination of in 1909, 27; and Plan of San Diego, 57

Cananea: population of, 12; strike at, 15

Carranza, Venustiano: support of by Gompers and Wilson, xiii; death of, 8; as characterized by Flores Magón, 51; support of by Gompers, 53; use of antilabor tactics by, 54; political use of bor-

Designer:	U.C. Press Staff
Compositor:	Prestige Typography
Text:	10/12 Palatino
Display:	Palatino
Printer:	Haddon Craftsmen
Binder:	Haddon Craftsmen